MW00616185

JUMPSTART YOUR CHILDCARE SUCCESS

7 Millionaire Secrets to Fast Enrollment,
Mainstream Marketing, Parent Attraction,
Staff Retention, Abundance and More

LaShon Carter

Copyright © 2021 LaShon Carter

All rights reserved.
No part of this book may be reproduced or used in any manner without the
prior written permission of the copyright owner, except for the use of brief
quotations in a book review. To request permissions, contact the publisher
at iownadaycare1@gmail.com.

Paperback: 978-1-7373415-0-5
Hardback: 978-1-7373415-1-2

Printed by JS Press and Publishing in the USA.
JS Press and Publishing
jspressandpublishing@gmail.com

This book is dedicated to all of the
Child Care Bosses around the world.

INTRODUCTION

We Don't Get Ready, We Stay Ready!

Where did this book come from?

As with most child care business owners, it starts with having a love for children and it evolves into running a full service business that requires next level skill sets and strategies to stay on the cutting edge. Your next level is the sum of the top 5 people that you spend the most time with. As a result of what they know and experienced you then can glean from them and build yourself up. In this book you will gather a new network of childcare owners to glean from. These lessons have caused women to succeed beyond the norm and against all odds. I am excited about this project due to the fact of an old quote that says:

Teams Aren't Built In A Day, But They Are Built Each Day! Within this book you will hear from a team of childcare business owners who are built for greatness.

Every day we are provided motivation and inspiration from each other though one form of media or another and that's how we created this network.

Read through this book with a notepad and pencil and write down the methods, stories and systems that you can use and glean from.

Much to Your Success!
The Team!

CONTENTS

ABUNDANT

MINDSET

ONE DAY, ONE TOUCH, ONE WORD
AND ALL THINGS CHANGED

To have an Abundance Mindset, one must first desire it, want it and pursue it. Also, having that type of mindset will definitely require a change of one's thinking.

There are two types of thinking in Abundance you can have.

Abundance Mindset: where you think there is more out there for you.

Scarcity Mindset: where you think there's very little out there for you.

Both thoughts work, but as you think that is how it becomes in your life.

If you believe there's more out there then you will get more, so the question is, what do you want? Life gives you not what it has, but what you think.

Let me tell you about the day I shifted my thinking into an Abundance thinking Mindset.

While sitting at my corporate job where I had been employed for over 15 years, I had come to a place in my life where I was feeling an incompleteness within myself. I was feeling as though I wasn't in my true purpose. Just sitting behind a desk shuffling invoices all day wasn't the life I desired.

Now, I was a wife and a mother, who was daily pouring everything I had into their lives. Making sure they were okay and giving little time to myself.

One day, I said to myself, "Sheryl, is this what you want to do for the rest of your life?" Although I love being a wife and mother, I was still feeling unfulfilled. I was doing just what I had to do in those areas of my life. That's all I knew to do, was to take care of others; besides, that's all I knew growing up.

I felt there was so much more in me and for me, and that God had to have a much bigger plan for me. Have you ever had that feeling that there is more? Maybe you're going about your daily routine and it feels as if something is missing. You know that feeling down in your spirit that keeps nagging at you day and night. You even go to sleep with it, hoping it will go away, and you find yourself waking right back up with the same feeling. Trust me, I know the feeling, and we're going to get through this together, so keep reading.

I always wanted to be in a financially wealthy place, but where I was working only provided a good income and benefits. For some, that may have been all they wanted, *but I didn't* see myself getting what I thought was needed from working for someone else, building their empire.

I wanted to build something for myself and my family. I wanted to see my family succeed and gain wealth. I am sure you feel the same way, hence why you're reading this chapter. No worries, I am going to walk this out with you.

I continued to work my 8-5 job. I began to think of other things I enjoyed doing, and that was caring for others, especially children. Even though I had my own children, I found myself always caring for others whether they were relatives or other people's children. So, in me questioning and seeking God for clarity in what I should do, I heard "daycare". Now when that hit my spirit I felt so surprised. I said to myself "God, is that what you're saying? Start a childcare business?

But just like you, I ignored what God said and continued to think of other ways to be successful. But for some reason, daycare kept coming back to me. How can starting a daycare be a way of gaining success and Abundance? I said to myself, there were a few other things I liked doing also. Then I started taking childcare classes even while working my corporate job. I completed them and stepped out on faith and started my own family home childcare business.

It was a great success. In my very first complete year of doing business, I made over $50,000 dollars. I want you to imagine starting your childcare business and "BAM!", God blows on it and you're successful in your very first year.

That's how I felt. I believe I made the right decision in faith. I then thought this could be bigger, but just opening up a business was not easy at all. I just knew that I could not be a small thinker in opening and running a whole center. I often questioned myself, "Do I really have what it takes?"

My thinking about myself was small minded; therefore, my thinking of business was small too. Over and over in my mind I kept asking myself, "Do you have what it takes?"

There weren't many positive-speaking people in my life. I had people that loved me, but business minded thinkers, there was only one. A. Maurice Maddox, my brother. He was my greatest inspiration when it came to business. He was the one with the degrees in business and was very successful in it. He would always say to me, "Put your mind to it, Sheryl." And I would keep saying, "but it requires so much more than a family home business." Again, here goes that small minded thinking. He would often tell me that if I gave people what they wanted and kept it professional, then I would always have clients and not customers for my business.

There was no one at that time teaching on Abundance thinking. For many that are being reared in church, that frame of thinking just was not taught.

My mind definitely needed a shift of thinking.

So after running my family home childcare business for five years, I stepped out in my faith once again and opened my first childcare center. And again, it was a success.

I'm really starting to look at this more of the Abundance Life.

I had to let go of the comfortable things that I knew for sure would take care of where I was now. I had to start to embrace and go after creative thinking that would cause my life to shift.

So now I began thinking it's all in my thinking and if I just allowed for my mindset to change about the way I see business, then I could think bigger. I then began to gain so much more confidence in myself, so now within the first five years of opening my first center, I now had opened three childcare centers.

Now, running and operating one childcare center is enough for some, but I then was able to see that if I would just only multiply what I had done for the first one, then I could do the same and gain more. Again, my thinking was taking another leap of faith.

I then felt that as long as I could change my mind to a new way of thinking in Abundance, then I could attain anything I wanted or desired. I could then see how this thinking could bring wealth into my family.

I began thinking of ways of setting myself in a place of an Abundance Mindset. I felt it was important for my life, family, and business success.

But not only to think of having an Abundance, but how to create it also.

I even started placing myself around abundant-minded thinking people, others that were thinking like I was, making statements of confession for my life and business, but mostly believing in myself that I was created for this. Now, was this easy? Not at all. I had to first figure out why I was thinking this way and what was keeping me from obtaining it. And who was to blame for not having it. I had to have a real look in the mirror. And what the reflection was showing me, was "Me". It wasn't that someone was keeping it from me, but I just didn't know how to get it.

I even had to check my circle of friends and associates. I found myself carrying on the same bad spirits as my circle. I didn't like that at all. For example "While working on my corporate job I became upset about something and I said a curse word. Remember I grew up in the church and using bad language was not a part of my vocabulary. I immediately checked myself" I knew at that very moment I had become a product of my circle of influence.

You see when you start to change your circle your language must be nsync with those you're around. Positive thinkers must always be thinking of unlimited opportunities for business.

I had to start guarding my mind, in a way. I had to watch what I was hearing and what I would allow myself to be around. I didn't want to come off as pushing folks away, but I just knew that if I allowed negative thoughts or people in my presence, it would not help me move forward. So that might even mean sometimes editing some things you are doing from close family because they will not always see what you see or believe what you believe.

I also learned that I would have to invest more into myself if I wanted this type of Abundance.

So, I started attending as many childcare conferences as I could that were talking about success and Abundance. I even made investments in books, tapes, and even invested in having a coach.Sometimes you have to bring others in to help you attain the frame of mind that's needed to help you shift your thinking. But it must be the right person.

So now that I have shifted my way of thinking of my life and business, I have learned the many strategies to have an Abundance Mindset. I've also learned that you must Embrace it. People who can do that believe there's plenty for everyone and don't mind sharing it. And they also will be willing to share how they accomplished the Abundance in their lives. And then when you have the mindset to expand, this will lead to gaining wealth in your life and business.

With you having an Abundance Mindset, you don't go around thinking how small something is, but how big you can make it.

So, you must stay positive and ask yourself what frame of mindset must I have to create an Abundance Mindset?

Now, this way of thinking does come with a cost.

Sometimes, this may cause some inconvenience in your life. You may have to give up something, give up some sleep and even some fun, and enjoyable things. You must have a plan for Abundance in your life. You have to identify your current limiting belief, then you have to see what is really causing you to think the way you are thinking. But when you find out how your limiting belief system is really costing you, then this is when you can really shift to an Abundance Mindset.

But first, you can't move past what was first holding you back from thinking in Abundance, and you must surround yourself with a group of people that can and will inspire you to stay in an unlimited mind of thinking, ones that will challenge you and hold you accountable, and sometimes, even this comes at a cost.

Below I want to share with you my Seven Step Abundance Mindset Method. These are the same methods I used when I first started on my childcare journey and let me tell you these methods changed my life and business. I want you to experience the same. Here's what I want you to do.

1. Grab a pen and paper and as you read each method write them down.

2. Write at the top of your paper the date and time you're reading these methods. Writing the date and time will signify your date of commitment.

3. Make a commitment to yourself that from this point on you will become in charge of your life.

Here is my Seven Step Abundance Mindset Method below:

1. Expand your Gratitude.
2. Surround yourself with Abundance-minded people.
3. Create a Life of Abundance.
4. Focus more time on what you love to do.
5. Follow your Passion.
6. Build a life of Abundance.
7. Expand Abundance and eliminate Scarcity.

Method 1. Expand Your Gratitude.

"Grateful people practice proactive gratitude."

Each day I gave God the thanks for being where I was at the moment. Life wasn't perfect, but I believe that the more grateful I became, the more God expanded my business. You have to wake up each day with the intention to be grateful. Remember, this is something you should do every day, and be consistent. Not only should you be grateful for where you are now, but show gratitude to God for where you are going.

Method 2. Surround Yourself With Abundance-minded People.

"Build your network of like-minded people."

This is something I had to do over time. I knew I had to change my circle to more positive and influential people. One of the ways I did that was to first become that Abundance-minded person. When you work on yourself first, God has a way of connecting you with the people you need and desire. It will seem uncomfortable in the beginning because it's not always easy leaving what is familiar, but remember, in order to get to where God desires you to be, you must be uncomfortable.

Method 3: Create a Life of Abundance.

"Having an abundance mindset is believing that you are created as more than enough, you have more than enough and more than enough is coming to you in the future" Scott Epp

I first began to have a heart of Gratitude, always thankful for where I was and seeing the Miracles of God's grace upon me. I began to see myself and believe I was worthy of the type of lifestyle I wanted. (I had to believe it, before it manifested.) I stopped making excuses and blaming others. I made a sincere commitment to myself that I would look for opportunities that would cause me to always be thinking and living "Abundance."

Method 4: Focus More Time on What You Love to Do — Be Creative.

"Doing what you love is the cornerstone of having abundance in your life. "Wayne Dyer"

Since childcare was what I loved doing , I just knew that this gift God had given me was something I truly loved doing, but it was also given to prosper me. And if I could find ways of being more creative in my childcare business, it would make room for me. So I looked at other ways childcare services were needed for parents.

Providing services outside the normal working hours, providing virtual Learning Time for working parents, and providing take-home learning education tools.

Now in having this type of Abundance in my business and my life, I knew I had to stay focused and in a positive environment at all times. If I came in contact with anyone speaking negatively or the conversation was not to enhance me, I would quickly change the conversation or remove myself from it.

Method 5: Follow Your Passion — How Much Time Are You Spending on What You Love?

"Follow your passion it will lead you to your purpose" Oprah

I found myself so passionate about my business that I literally found myself going to sleep and waking up with my business on my mind. I would constantly think about childcare and how I could become better each day. I just knew that I had to dedicate as much of my time as I could to see all my dreams be fulfilled.

I also knew that I would be challenged from time to time, but that I would tackle whatever challenges I would face.

Never giving up, I learned how to value my time and to do the things that I loved and that would bring me a great return. I found that I also had to prioritize things in my life.

Method 6: Build a Life of Abundance Thinking—Be an Abundance Mindsetter.

"The debts of your abundance depends on the debts of your gratitude" Unknown

I chose to think with a positive mindset and be more grateful for all that God was doing in my life. I looked at ways that would cause me to think this way. I started attending many business conferences in childcare and other networking events. I would place things within my daily view (vision boards), seeing these things for my life. I would also look for all the resources available to me. I started reading books on how successful people think. Well, you might be thinking, why would you have to learn to think the way successful people think? Because when you learn how to change the way you think, it will bring you so much more knowledge, you will also learn that it will also generate revenue and help solve many problems. This way of thinking will also create many other great opportunities. It can take you to a whole new level personally and professionally. It can literally change your very life.

You must also invest in yourself. Find yourself a coach or mentor, someone who could help you get to where you desire to go.

You must have a plan for Abundance in your life. Always remain in an unlimited mind of thinking, one that will always challenge you and hold you accountable.

I would also plan for rest time, take vacations so that I could get rejuvenated, so when I would return home, I would feel spiritually and physically stronger. "I enjoyed my Me Time."

I even had to cut off some fun things I like to do and even decline many family fun times. It was hard but I knew I had to step out of my comfort zone to receive the greater rewards God had just for me.

**Method 7: Expand Abundance and Eliminate Scarcity—
Focus on Your Existing Strengths.**

"The key to abundance is to meet limited circumstances with unlimited thoughts" Marianne Williamson

I would no longer say I can't. There is no place for fear, but instead, focus on expanding your existing strengths.

You must get much clarity to your vision and goals you want for yourself. And to know that if you think of yourself in this Abundance Mindset.

If you live your life by expressing gratitude daily, you will then begin to feel the Abundance increase in your life.

Finally, You must look at things now with, how can I make them "Bigger" with my Abundance Mindset? This will cause you again to come out of being in your comfort zone.

So are you ready to choose to have the Abundance Mindset and have more of it for your life?

Congratulations! You have now completed the "Abundance Mindset Method."

I am so proud of you! Give yourself a pat on the back!

My prayer is that you have a new way of thinking and you take all of the tools I have given you to create the life you desire. I want you to know that I am here for you and will be with you every step of the way. Because of the shift of the way I think God has given me so much fulfillment and wealth. And I want the same for you!

Now it is time to put in some action! Which method will you commit to working on first? Once you've made your commitment it's now time for accountability. Email me at: sheryl4god1@yahoo.com and let me know which method you are committed to first and we will continue the journey together.

Keep believing and keep achieving and remember your new life and business starts with the way you "Think".

ABOUT THE AUTHOR

Sheryl Lovett is the CEO of Alpha Bright Children Learning Center, LLC in the city of Lakeland, Florida

Where she owns and operates multiple childcare facilities, she has been in the childcare business for over 19 years.

She is also the owner of Anointed Savory, a catering company that prides the savory flavor of seasoning with Love.

She is also the Co-Owner of Elegant Affairs of Lakeland, an event planning company, where they bring "Elegance" to any event.

In the upcoming months Sheryl will be launching her Childcare Consulting firm, where she will be empowering men and women to go after their dreams and passion in life.

Sheryl is a true believer that age is nothing but a number, and where she sees herself as not retiring. but just getting started.

Sheryl has been married to the love of her life James Lovett Sr for over 39 yrs. She's a mother of 5 successful blessed children Lanora, Shayla, James (Leon) Demetruis and Taiquila. Grandmother of 10.

Sheryl serves as an Ordained Mother of her church The Greater New Hope Ministry of Plant City, Florida under the Leaders Pastor Calvin Callins and Dr .Tandria Callins

Sheryl, also known as Mother Sheryl internationally, serves as the Moderator of the Jumpstart Your Day Prayer Line for Childcare Business owners around the world, under the leadership of Pastor Kamau Dickerson and First Lady/Coach Andrea Dickerson.

FROM TERMINATION TO DETERMINATION, THE SAFE TAKEOVER

"Just kill your kids, and you won't have to be late for our Friday morning meetings!" he said. John, the general manager, started laughing so hard that he had his right hand on his big belly, and his left knee touched the ground where my mind had told me to knock him down. It was at this moment I thought I couldn't breathe. It was at this moment, I just wanted to leave. It was at this moment that God truly spoke to me. I stood there for what seemed like an eternity because I was still trying to process the direct, derogatory statement that the general manager expressed to his top sales manager of the furniture business I had grinded so hard for.

After coming back to reality from the voice of the Holy Spirit, I immediately grabbed my Bible out of my drawer and ran quickly to the restroom where I stayed for the entire duration of my eight-hour shift. I remember several customers and employees attempting to get inside the restroom but for some reason, I just couldn't come out! I cried and cried until I couldn't even see any words in my Bible due to tears that poured down my face to the pages that I was trying to read in order to gain strength to open the door. I didn't know how to feel or what to do. I knew the devil was on a loose path and I had to get out and stay out of the way. I did make my way out through the scripture in James 4:7; Submit yourselves, then, to God. Resist the devil, and he will flee from you (NIV).

The next three weeks were very rough with me attempting to sell anything. Because I stood up to the enemy, with the scriptures, I was terminated from my sales management position on Oct 22. I knew this was going to happen because I started wearing my Armored Uniform to work. After getting the Good News of being released from my work duties, I gathered my personal belongings and went to get in my car. I just remember sitting while thinking, and spoke out Loud to God, what's next? Just sitting still and quiet with only my breath, I CLEARLY heard the Holy Spirit whisper, "When you go back to work it's gonna be for your own corporation." Not knowing what this really meant, I continued sitting in silence in the parking lot of the company that had just terminated me, until my phone rang. I answered and my sister was saying she needed me to care for her kids today while she went to handle some business. She didn't know that I was at work, but just now, out of work. I agreed and told her I needed about one hour to get myself together. Meeting up with her later led to my eagerness to want to help her get a job, go back to school, and complete goals to take care of her children. That same day I was terminated, I used determination to safely care for my nephews for Free! Yes, I said Free!

I didn't know what I know now, but for the next two years, I faithfully and safely nurtured my sister's four children from the heart in our home. I had a side hustle or two that helped over the time until unemployment benefits ran out. I just knew God was able to continue providing, so I asked the Lord about what I could do to help my family. God told me that I was already doing it! While sitting there thinking, what am I doing? I was reminded that the termination from the last job was supposed to be used as determination for my next job. The next time you go back to work, it would be for your own corporation! Wow! My mind was going places where my thoughts needed to be, so I jumped up and went to my home office to start my research. I learned quickly that I AM already operating a business in the childcare industry and I just needed to safely certify it. Learning about licensing a home, regulations, and getting money to do what I already was currently doing sparked so much determination in my life, which caused me to go into overdrive.

Like most of you, Loving on children becomes naturally fit for our lives if we have children of our own or are around them regularly. I've always cared for and nurtured children that came across my path. Now was the time to earn and build from what I already had been doing.

Our home was licensed as a family childcare home for up to twelve children, with an approved assistant, within twenty-four hours after my initial inspection. My husband had painted the garage and built some steps, and we called our licensing representative out and she went ahead and certified us, just like that. We operated our family business twenty-four hours, seven days per week to offer flexibility for families who had children. From my last experience with corporate America, I was determined to create flexibility for working families who had children that needed to be attended to safely while meeting demands of corporate rules and family goals.

Other families heard about the flexibility that our home setting provided. We soon had to expand from our personal home to renting another home to conduct childcare for the community. An opportunity presented to me to rent another home directly across the street helped me understand God's plan a little more as I handled closing the deal to prepare for our second childcare home. Definitely not the easiest task, since the State Department had never experienced any of what was happening with licensing two childcare homes operated from another location other than personal home settings. I kept referencing the words that I clearly heard God speak on the day I was terminated. "When you go back to work, it will be for your own corporation." Already, I had learned how to operate our childcare homes like a real business, so I knew God was setting me up to run a corporation like it was spoken to me back in Oct 2009. Learning systems about the specific industry of childcare helped me scale to the corporate scene. I learned from Andrea, America's #1 Child-care Success Coach with I Own A Daycare that I didn't have to recreate the wheel.

We opened our first twenty-four-hour, six-day weekly childcare facility in November 2016, with a second location to have our children experience a safe start before and after school in Aug 2018. "Our community is only as strong as the people who live in it" I thought of when I created a non-profit organization called Safe Care Communities in the middle of the worst health crisis turned pandemic in October 2020. From Termination to Determination, The Safe Takeover is just Beginning.

I'm a parent of four and now a grandmother of six. I am an expert at many things, but my #1 expertise I pride myself on is being a mother to my children. I knew what my family needed in order for me to take care of them. The only way I was able to work anywhere was because I demanded flexibility with my employer due to my obligations and responsibilities as a parent first! While working for corporate America, I had to compromise so much of my family's growth for the growth of an organization who suggested I harm my children, just to listen to sales tips and uncomfortable language at the Friday morning meetings.

My three ultimate success tips to jumpstart your childcare business success is to: 1. Manage and provide flexibility for enrollments. 2. Build meaningful relationships. 3. Keep a professional attitude at all times! When parents, businesses, and other organizations are confident that these three are on the table, this can ultimately help them make a decision faster to choose your program or business to provide childcare services for their family.

Enrolling families for me is simple. I listen to what they describe as their family needs and create a system of programming for their requests. This is all a part of wanting to have a relationship with your families or clients well enough to help recognize their childcare needs and targeting solutions, because they really are depending on you. Fast enrollments happen due to responding to their needs faster.

Just recently, I was out of town having a strategy session with my childcare coach. No matter how much I think I know about childcare, my coach keeps me on the cutting edge with mainstream marketing strategies, enrollments, parent attractions, and more. As I continue learning to increase my social media presence to market my business, I had some down time while our flight was delayed due to rough weather conditions. Scrolling through one of the local childcare groups on social media, I see a post from a mother seeking third-shift childcare. Responding to the post with our available services, flexibility was the key selling point that needed to be highlighted. Another member wanted to chime in with negative, derogatory lies about our center and the service she was provided. This person wanted to cause discord for no reason. Her children never attended our center, like she stated, and I was able to provide a very real respectful, positive and professional response to the individual. I stated that I am the CEO, owner, and director of the childcare center you are attempting to assassinate, and I'm confident that you are typing things that are not true. I went on to let the young lady know that I knew each and every one of my parents' names and their children who had previously come and left, and even the ones who are currently happy with our service, and your name or your pictures of your family are not in our business database.

Just from this social site post, our center gained 10 new enrollments. How? Because we use the **"The Safe Care Method."**

1. **Safe Flexibility** - Families, employees, and the community need partnerships with childcare centers who are willing to meet them where they are.

Examples of flexibility for families:

- Number of hours in attendance
- Split shifts or varied shifts
- Extended care for childcare
- Payment arrangements
- Create a scholarship program
- Create discount incentives

Examples of flexibility for employees:

- Flexible work schedules with proper notice (make sure this is stated in your Employee Handbook)
- Mentorship programs
- Overtime for family program
- Flexible childcare services and discounts

Examples of flexibility for employers:

- Partnership with flexibility to increase productivity
- Barter service/exchange marketing advertisement cycles
- Support local employment with open childcare slots availability

2. **Safe Relationships** - Building the trust:

- Know families, children, and employees by name
- Responsive to the needs of the childcare market
- Advocacy with knowledge

3. **Professionalism** - Self-awareness, purposeful development

- Continuous professional development
- Belief in diversity and inclusion
- Dedication to treating everyone fair

Some of the same safe strategies mentioned above caused me to go from termination to determination for the creation, growth, and success of my organization, which resulted in The Safe Takeover:

- Starting a childcare business from home.
- Expanding our business to two other in-home childcare businesses.
- Expanding to a 24/6 childcare facility.
- Opened a second center, before and after school program.
- Created a non-profit organization.

Although I was terminated from a position that I believed was secured, my inspiration that I received from God on the same day was what led me From My Termination to My Determination to Safely Take Over the Childcare Industry!

S-Secure
A-Applied
F-Flexibility
E-Enrollment

C-Create
A-Approaches
R-Relationship
E-Experience

ABOUT THE AUTHOR

Kimberly Kemp is a real serious, serial entrepreneur and founder of a non-profit organization with the mission to continue serving families, children and the community. For more than two decades, Kimberly has served as a Safe Support for the children and their families' overall growth with a whole family approach. She's been called upon by many to consult and coach life and business strategies to increase value for their lives. Through continual efforts to create partnerships with local and national organizations, she has the determination to bring advocacy to the forefront for flexibility in the sector for working families.

Kimberly attended Kaplan University, where she received her Business Management Degree.

She has successfully created, managed and operated several childcare home businesses with such great success that it caused her to pursue a Safe Takeover in the Childcare Industry. Really serious about entrepreneurship, she has continued growth, with success, while operating two childcare centers with plans of creating a Safe Enterprise.

Kimberly is a wife to a very supporting husband, a mother of four and grandmother of six.

Kimberly brings her unique, natural ability to simplify the complexity of our thoughts to experience real results!

Contact Information:
Kimberly Kemp, Handle Business 4ME, Consulting
www.safecare4kids.center
kkempsafecare@gmail.com
info@hb4me.com
(B) 319-233-0889
(F) 1-866-522-0810
Facebook: safecarelearning

PARENT ATTRACTION
METHOD

HOW I BUILT MY BUSINESS AND GREAT RELATIONSHIPS IN A BIG CITY

My family emigrated from Trinidad, West Indies to America, and upon arriving I remember my mom saying that she was rich. Didn't quite feel that way though, as we moved into a two-bedroom apartment in a building and not the house that I believed rich people lived in. Little did I know that her definition of being rich was having her children close to her, as we had been separated for a few years before. She was an extremely hard worker and always put her children first. I fondly remember the little things that my mom would do, like never hanging up the telephone without saying that she loved me, which she still does to this day. I learned from her early on that being rich was much more than the amount of money that you possessed. It was about the relationships that you built with people that were more valuable.

"Life isn't a matter of milestones, but of moments." - Rose Kennedy

I was fourteen years old when I got my first taste of the American dream. I was given the opportunity to work after school at a childcare center. My first boss, Ms. Lucille, was no different from my mom. A hard worker in the childcare industry, she was always loving and kind to her staff, the parents, and the children in her care. I loved how she interacted with her parents, and how they spoke freely around her. I saw their dedication to her program as well, as they were involved in many activities at the center. Observing her over the years, I was reminded often of the things that my mom had taught me. I was learning parent attraction techniques from these two women and didn't even know it.

I remember when I took the leap and opened my first childcare center almost twenty years ago. My brother brought me to the site because he saw a sign that read "childcare center available." I had never been to that neighborhood, I knew no one there, and I had never run a childcare center before, but I wasn't nervous, because what I did have was my love for children and a way of drawing others to me. Now... How would I, a small child care center in New York City, attract parents to my program? One thing that I knew to be true was that I never wanted to lose my focus of education and love being a priority. Love was the main ingredient, and I had learned that from both my mom and Ms. Lucille. Well, I also had faith because after all, New York City was the concrete jungle where dreams were made of, right?

I opened my center in June of 2001, and enrolled my first child within two weeks. Even with two children, one being my nephew, I ran my program as though I was full and operated as a large childcare facility. I complied with all requirements, I made sure that all academic assignments and extracurricular activities were completed, sent home newsletters, catered meals, and even went on school trips.

I began to pay close attention to the needs in the area. In addition to ensuring that my fees were affordable, I noticed that parents needed a program that operated a little later than 6:00pm. I decided to open until 7:00pm, and I advertised by handing out flyers in the neighborhood and at local schools. I also placed flyers in deli's and at the library in the area. In a few short months, my center went from two children to being full to capacity.

I've always been a creative child, and that has assisted me in business as well. After two years in business, and before many places were renting out their centers for events, I began doing so as a way to earn extra income. It all began when a parent whom I had a good relationship with asked to have her child's party after school one day because her apartment was very small. I worked a second job in those days and was worried about leaving my center open when I was not there. I suggested that she have the party on a Saturday evening so that I could be there to monitor the event. She gladly accepted the offer. The party went well and soon I was renting for events every weekend. We were booked with children's parties, baby showers, christenings, and other events. My brother quickly stepped in and began helping by setting up for the events and cleaning up the space in preparation for school on Mondays. Eventually I had to hire someone to do the job.

I saw people bringing in balloons and decorating the center for their events, and the wheels started turning in my head. I took balloon decorating classes and began to offer that service as well. I was decorating almost every weekend, and not only at the center. I enjoyed it and even began renting tables and chairs for the events. It grew into a full event services business with me also teaching others to decorate. Soon, our space would also be used in the evenings for business meetings and church events. My office became full with contracts and business cards for more than four businesses. What an exciting and busy time that was.

As time passed, I realized that life as a childcare owner in New York City was no small feat. Things move super fast, childcare centers pop up two and three on a block, and the rules and regulations are more rigorous and burdensome than smaller cities. The cost of living is high, meaning employees require higher compensation in order to live. It also means that the cost of doing business is higher. The requirements for staff also make it difficult to run a successful business. Many of our programs require master's degrees and state certifications for lead staff. Oftentimes, these challenges made it difficult to maintain clientele as well.

With all of the big city hardships, one thing that I do have in common with many entrepreneurs is that we don't find comfort at one level because we are always seeking knowledge and the opportunity to grow. We are resilient, and I learned early on that in order for my business to survive, I needed to make changes, invest in myself and in my business, and incorporate new ways of attracting and retaining clients. I was determined not to let my challenges keep me from my goals. I remember organizing my office to incorporate color-coded file folders. This made finding things in the office very easy and it looked awesome too. The postings on the walls were neat, and I created checklists for everything with dates on when things should be done or should be corrected. When anyone walked into my space they appreciated the attention to detail. I also sought knowledge by looking for a childcare coach, and found Coach Andrea Dickerson. By purchasing her material and incorporating what I learned, I saw my business not just begin to grow but to thrive. I created systems, effective staff training, learned additional ways to increase my parent attraction skills, and learned marketing techniques. I also remembered lessons learned from my mom and Ms. Lucille, and I remembered that I was a pro at parent attraction.

That was when I created my **P.A.R.E.N.T.** Attraction Method.

P - Preparation: In order to have a great childcare business you must always be prepared.

As parents came in to inquire about the program, there were a few things that I made sure were always done. I made sure that they were always greeted with a warm smile and that there were lots of registration packets and handouts available. I made sure that the center was always clean and organized. I was always prepared to tell them about our history, our motto and vision, tell them what our center had to offer, and answered any questions that they had. I also enlightened my team on questions that parents had, so they would be prepared with answers if ever asked.

A - Attraction: Find creative ways to attract clients.

Attract your clients by focusing on the needs in your community and be open and ready to implement them. Adjust your opening and closing times if needed. Distribute flyers and use social media as a form of marketing and advertising. Host events and always have business cards and flyers on hand. One simple technique that I used was calling everyone mom, dad, grandma, grandpa, aunty, and uncle. It made them comfortable with me and our program, and also gave that personal touch. To this day, almost twenty years later, I still use this technique.

R - Revenue: Incorporating multiple streams of income within your childcare business not only brings in extra income but helps bring parents and families into your facility.

What are you passionate about? Use that to increase your revenue and attract parents into your business. My event business allowed me to market my childcare business to anyone who walked through my doors. I gave parents who booked for children's parties a $100 voucher for my childcare service. Our school fundraisers, while bringing in extra revenue, also allowed me to attract new clients by giving out vouchers and other incentives to participants.

E - Education: Make education a priority. Create a unique curriculum and keep educating yourself as your business grows.

This allows you to offer more to your parents and they will see the value in your program. Always let parents know how important education is to you and the role it plays in your program. Let them know how they can contribute to their child's learning experience. Also continue to educate yourself and your team. Let your parents know about your team's educational accomplishments and how they are becoming masters of their craft. Also offer classes to support parent learning. For example, create a parent university, GED classes, resume writing classes, and network with other companies to provide needed resources and information to help families.

N - Never Lose Yourself: Be authentic.

Parents will enroll their child or children into your program because of this. Know your WHY. I love reading and that is told to parents looking to enroll their child and it is woven into my daily curriculum. Always stay true to yourself and you will attract your ideal client.

T - Teachers: Educate your staff on your program so that they can assist in attracting clients.

Teachers play an important role in your program's success. Your staff should know how to greet parents and how to convey messages to them. They should also show love to the children. I have learned that my team is a representation of me, so I ensure through staff training that they are equipped with the skills needed to help the children succeed and to again assist and include the parents and families in any way possible.

I knew that parents appreciated the love that their children received at our centers, so that became a main focus. To this day, my students get hugs and words of encouragement often. I also include my parents by featuring them in the school's monthly newsletter and even have them join our different event committees. We post on our school's website and our school's social media page often to keep them engaged. We have trivia activities for our parents and even involve them in things that are happening at our centers. All of this creates a positive school environment and increases parent involvement. (Research shows that parents who are involved in their school's community tend to have children who do better at school.) It's a win-win for everyone.

I also learned the importance of community involvement. In addition to community involvement projects that we do often, I ensure that I have a good relationship with the neighborhood schools and teachers that are in the lives of my school-age children. Whatever I can do to help my students succeed is important to me, and the principals and teachers appreciate our involvement and concern. They are always willing to work with us and most importantly, recommend us to parents.

By incorporating my parent attraction methods, I have not only filled one center, but have gone on to opening and operating three childcare facilities. In addition to my preschool programs, school-age programs and summer camp, I am also a children's book author and run my company, Storytime Readers. With the slogan "Storytime is Funtime, it's a storytelling business that brings fun to children through reading." It also allows me the opportunity to promote my childcare business. As you will notice, all of my businesses are built around children and, of course, love. I have no intention of losing any part of myself. Not even New York City with its hustle and bustle lifestyle can take that from me. I've learned to differentiate myself without losing myself.

Today, I am proud of where I've been, what I've learned, and where I'm going. I am well on my way to becoming, as my mom would say, "rich." I'm growing a childcare empire built on love. *My ultimate definition of success.*

I pray that when I am no longer here, that I have blessed the lives of the many children and families that have crossed my path. Though millionaire status is great, love is greater. If Covid-19 has taught me anything, it has taught me the meaning of life and love.

Childcare Bosses, you too can live out your life's purpose despite the many challenges that you may face. Find your strength and passion, and use them to grow your business and build great relationships with clients.

Connect with me at thecoconutgrovecec@outlook.com and tell me what P.A.R.E.N.T. Attraction Method tips you're incorporating. Be sure to give me your feedback.

So now, jumpstart your childcare program today. Get those parents in the doors and let them fall in love with your program.

"The only way to do great work is to love what you do."–Steve Jobs

ABOUT THE AUTHOR

Leslie-Ann Mason has been involved in the early childhood industry for over thirty years; volunteering, teaching and working with children in various environments including kindergarten, private preschools, school-age programs, and city funded child care centers.

After graduating from college, Leslie-Ann worked two full-time jobs with the dream of one day opening a childcare center. Almost twenty years ago she opened her first childcare center. She is the founder and CEO of **The Coconut Grove Childhood Education Center, Inc.** a group of childcare centers in Brooklyn, New York. Her mission is to assist in the transformation of children's lives and in the industry of early childhood education by offering a nurturing environment, the most up to date materials and resources, insightful conversations and connections through the power of her relationships with clients and the community that she serves.

She is also the proud owner of **Storytime Readers, Inc.,** a reading company that promotes reading in young children with the goal of making reading both educational and fun. Her love for children and her community is also evident in her company **Party Bear, Inc.,** a party delivery service that strives to put smiles on the faces of children. Party items are delivered to homes, schools, hospitals and anywhere that children are.

In addition to operating more than one childcare facility and her child related businesses, she is also an author and operates a not-for-profit organization that gives scholarships to students entering college, predominantly within the West Indian community. She has a true passion for community service, and serves as a member of many local and national organizations. One being her beloved sorority, Delta Sigma Theta Sorority, Incorporated. She enjoys the steel pan community, all genres of music, dancing, decorating and organizing, cleaning, and DIY projects.

Over the years she has created many signature events, from Thanksgiving dinners, to an annual Spring Fling Event which garners more than five hundred children and families from the community.

Leslie-Ann enjoys helping other childcare bosses excel as well, and is passionate about systems and organization in the child-care industry. She has become known for her ability to create a loving family environment in all of her childcare programs. Her understanding of the importance of love is obvious in her personal and professional life.

FAST ENROLLMENT
METHOD

"HOW TO GO FROM TWENTY-EIGHT TO STAYING OPEN LATE."

"There is no force equal to a woman determined to rise." (W.E.B. Dubois)

Let me take you back to September 2018. My childcare business was suffering one of the hardest blows since opening in 2015. My rent was four months behind and I only had twenty-eight kids enrolled. With the time clock ticking, I only had 30 days to reach my capacity of 116 kids.

As I sat in my office with my head in my hands, I knew I had to make a change in my enrollment FAST! In my story, you will learn all about not only how I overcame this hard blow but I will also give you my millionaire processes, systems, thought process, and mindset. So, go grab your favorite drink, sit back, and take notes of the seven secrets I am going to give you to help your enrollment FAST!

But first, let me tell you a little bit about me. My name is LaShon Carter from Chattanooga, TN. I went from working in childcare in 2008 at the age of twenty-one, to owning my own home daycare at the age of only twenty-eight. I didn't grow up with the blueprint of knowing how to start and grow a successful childcare business. But over the years, I've fallen down and gotten back up over and over again, never giving up, hence why you're reading this chapter. I can hear the late singer Aaliyah Haughton singing:

"And if at first you don't succeed, then dust yourself off and try again.

You can dust it off and try again."

Before I move forward, let me tell you a little truth. I did not want to leave my job. I loved my job where I was working. I worked as a seven up merchandiser, but all I could talk about at my job was owning my own childcare center one day. I would read books and listen to audio about childcare.

I remember getting some bad news from the doctors, telling me I had three large hernias that would kill me if I continued to do the job that I loved. I remember sitting in my house wondering what I was going to do for work. Then, a parent from the former childcare job I once worked at came to my doorstep with two beautiful kids, asking me if I could watch her kids so she could go to a job interview. I told her, sure, I would love to watch her children for her this one time. She came back excited about her job interview, and she was blessed to get the job the same day. On March 5th, 2015, I started my home daycare with two beautiful kids, then two kids became seven kids, and seven kids became 24 kids, and that was when I knew it was time for me to branch out and get my center. If I could enroll like this, I knew when I got my center, I would be big time.

Fast forward to January 2017, I was in full enrollment. I had so much love from the community, I was able to finally pay myself, and I could say I was really happy. Then in September 2018, as you guessed, my enrollment started to decrease. I was sitting in my office with my hands in my lap, trying to figure out what to do. My rent was behind four months and my enrollment was down. I knew I had to do something fast, and sitting in my office was not going to get it done. I felt the fear and dusted it off and got to work. Anytime you feel fear, allow yourself to feel and dust yourself off and get to work.

Let me share with you my seven secrets that helped me build my enrollment from twenty-eight to staying open late. I know that when you have the faith and the desire to grow your enrollment and you match that with your actions, you will not FAIL!

Grab your pen and paper and let's get to work.

Write this down: **The Seven Millionaire Enrollment Method**

1. Program benefits
2. Community Networking
3. Website and Branding
4. Social Media and Emailing
5. Partnership

6. Contribution to your program
7. Marketing

1. Program benefits

Ask yourself these questions.

1. Do I offer tutoring lessons?
2. Do I offer potty training?
3. Do I offer the best pre-K readiness program?
4. Do I offer night and weekend care?
5. Are my hours flexible?

I would advise you to take your benefits and add them to a flyer on your website and start sharing how your benefits can help your parents, or you can also share this with prior clients. Here are some of the things we do to enhance our parents' experience. We offer potty training, and with that, our parents learn and implement our top secrets to our potty-training class. These secrets can also be used at home. Down below, I want you to share some secrets about your program that your parents can use outside your program. Feel free to use my suggestions above.

_____

_____

_____

_____

2. Community Networking

Ask yourself, have I networked in the following areas in my community?

1.   Local business events
2.   Partnerships
3.   Warehouses/Hospitals
4.   Radio and newspaper ads
5.   Billboards

Community networks are so important. You must go outside your business and inside your community. What do they need from you as a business owner? Research your community that your business is in and see what local events happen each month. Look to partner with some other businesses in the community and do a trade with another business. We have done partnerships with local health care centers and cell phone and car dealerships that have helped with our increase in enrollment. Reach out to your local newspaper or radio broadcast and place an ad about your business and benefits. Offer something free for your community, do a yard sale or an open house event. When I was down in my enrollment, I remember walking my community and talking to families and other business owners who told me they did not need my services, and later called to partner with my business to help with staff that could not find care for their late work hours. I then realized I needed to add on later hours for the new warehouse jobs that were coming into my area. Find new businesses that are opening in your community that you can help with promoting their business and yours.

Down below, write out some ideas of how you could network in your community and grow your business.

_____

_____

_____

_____

3. Website and Branding

Ask yourself, what does my website say about my brand and business: Does it say boring, fun or exciting?

1. Tell a story with your website
2. Branding colors
3. Easy to navigate
4. Pictures and videos
5. Logo

A website speaks volume about your business. Having a website helps your clients understand your business and can help with questions about your services. When I asked my clients about my website they said it was easy to use and navigate, they can enroll from the site, make payments, and see pictures and videos of each classroom. Let your website tell a story about your business and what you offer (benefits). Even if they are not ready to sign up just yet, add them to your email list for when they are ready to sign up, or when you are ready to enroll, they will be ready.

Branding colors can help with enrollment, but too much color can kill a vibe. We have all seen where everyone uses either neutral colors or bright colors. In my program, I use bright colors and my parents are attracted to me by my bright colors. Let me tell you a little short story about how I came up with my daycare name. My great grandmother Ollie Pearl would call me tiger, beautiful and powerful and protector of her family but feared by many. I got my nickname Tiny from a friend, and it stuck so I took both names and put them together and named my childcare business Tiny Tigers, and my logo with the two tigers and the crayons made my logo pop. I rebranded myself by adding more colors to my logo. I attracted a family that was in town visiting family. They stopped by my childcare center thinking we had real tigers inside. I know right, but I turned that joke into a drop-in care enrollment when they were in town visiting family. Down below, I left you some room to write down some ideas on how you can improve your website and drive more people to enroll with you.

_____

_____

_____

_____

4. Social Media and Emailing

We all use social media and emailing to reach our new or potential parents, but are you using the right tools?

1. Posting at the right times
2. Facebook
3. Instagram
4. Email marketing
5. Testimonies

Social media posting can have your business phone ringing every day to where all your calls are regarding enrolling children. I post on my Facebook and Instagram page every day, going to each classroom posting about what is going on in the classroom. I also introduce new staff members that have joined our team. I mention new things we have purchased for the center and new partnerships we have formed within our community. Social media can help your business expand in so many ways. Add the call now button to where potential clients can call from Facebook to book an appointment with you from your business social media site.

Change your banner on your page every month. I started seeing a change in my business when I started posting more and going live on my Facebook in different classes. Everyone loves to have a fun time with toddlers. When I go inside my toddler program and play with the bubbles or we are singing our ABC's, we get so many views. Our parents share our videos and get their families to see and like the posts as well. We increase our enrollment by showing what we're doing inside our program. Take a look in your back office of your social media pages and look at what times people are viewing your posts and what things are getting the most likes or comments. That way, you can see what times you need to schedule your posts or go live.

I have seen that if you add testimonials to your page, you will have more people viewing your page as well as enrolling. Testimonials help with increasing your enrollment in your infant and toddler room. I have had parents add their testimonials onto the page from my infant program because that's the scary age to put your child in daycare. What is one thing most parents say? I don't want my child to start daycare until they can talk, so getting a testimony from one of my infant and toddler parents helps that parent that is scared to go to work change her mind, and she will call and book a tour, then either they will enroll or join your waiting list for your infant and toddler program. I still send out a newsletter to all my former parents. . When I do that, my intent is to get an enrollment or someone to email me back about how they can book a tour. This method helped me during September 2018 when I had low enrollment. I had a few parents disenroll and re-enroll once I sent out an email letting them know the new and exciting things that were going on in Tiny Tigers.

Below, write out some things that can help with your social media and email. Write down some parents you can ask for a few testimonials.

_____

_____

_____

_____

5. Partnership

When you think of partnership, who do you name? I am sure you're not thinking of the same people I am thinking of.

1. Chambers of Commerce
2. Banks
3. Call centers
4. Health care
5. **Early matter childcare**

Partnerships are exceptionally good for your business. Find some local businesses, like T-Mobile, AT&T, internet providers, hospitals, banks, warehouses, hospitality, fast food, recreation centers, and your local chamber of commerce. I have been with the Chattanooga Chamber of Commerce for a year and it has helped my business with marketing, business planning and budgeting, to speaking engagements, invites to special events, ribbon cuttings. The benefit of partnering with your local chamber of commerce is their network is huge, and you will meet so many other successful business owners that can help promote your business and move your business to higher levels.

I have enjoyed partnering with local businesses in my area. We take care of each other. I have partnered with many call centers in my area that have helped me increase my enrollment in my center to where I have a waiting list. I present the benefits of my company and ask the partner if any of my benefits will help inside their business. Don't worry about the no's, just keep going. I asked my local call center to post me on their job website for childcare, that we offer flexible hours and weekend care with no registration fee. Partnering up with local hospitals with their housekeeping staff when they are working late hours is a bonus as well. When other hospitals or hospitality services hear your benefits, your enrollment will go up.

I remember in my thirty days to fill up my center, I went from door to door of the business owners in my area, and everyone was either telling me no or we will reach back out to you. I walked into this health care facility and the lady was so excited to see me. It was as if she already knew me. She asked me my name and why did it take me so long to introduce myself. I laughed and smiled and said I had to build up the courage to come in. I gave her my business card and told her what my business benefits were. She smiled and told me, "I already know who you are. We've been waiting on you." Our partnership with this facility has been more than great. I am saying this to say, just because you get told no ten times, all it takes is courage and that eleventh door knock is your yes.

Start setting up a meeting with the hospitals and tell them what your benefits are and how your business can help, send them a thank you gift and some coupons for their staff. Do a follow-up call after every partnership and send out a nice thank you card to help them to pass on your business information. Ask yourself have you really reached out to your local businesses about what you can offer them and what they can offer you.

Below, make a list of people you could partner with, and get ready to knock on some doors.

_____

_____

_____

_____

6. Contribution to your program

Do you have a few people to thank that have contributed to your business? Here are a few tools I use to help me remember who I need to thank for helping my business grow.

1. Parents
2. Staff
3. Business owners
4. Coaches/Mentors
5. Volunteers

Do you have a few parents or staff business owners, coaches and mentors, and volunteers that have come and helped out at your local business? Hand out thank you notes or a nice gift to your parents, staff, business owners, mentors and coaches to show that you appreciate their services to your business. I remember a time in my business when one of my staff told me in a meeting that she felt unappreciated, that she felt like she does a great job and she shows up to work and she does all the training and more, and she felt overlooked, and I never knew that she felt that way. Ouch, that hurts don't it, when someone tells you that you don't show that you appreciate their services. Pick a day and show some love to your parents who bring their precious little ones to your business every day. Have some gift certificates from different businesses in your community. Have coffee with mom or dad and have a family day at your daycare. Have a day where your parents do a raffle and they win a prize or a free family meal on you.

Always celebrate your staff at least once a month with food for the entire staff, gift cards, gift certificates, day at the spa, car detail. Remember, you once worked for someone, so you wanted to feel important about your job and you wanted your job to see that you are a hard worker and you love your job. Your staff is coming to work each day to support your dream and to carry out your vision. Your parents should get coffee and muffins, or popcorn and juice. Find somewhere in your daycare where you can have a place to set up a nice meet and greet area for your parents to come and get a nice gift from you and your staff. I have a parenting class where they pick the topics and we discuss from budgeting tips to cleaning tips and cooking tips and home buying. This helps with showing I appreciate their services with me and my staff, and I am here to support your dreams as well. Celebrate your mentors/coaches that have contributed their time and given you great tips and wisdom to help you build that successful business. Send them a nice handwritten note thanking them for their services and advice in your business.

Below, write a list of people that have been helping you in your business and plan out something you would want to do for them.

_____

_____

_____

_____

7. Marketing

1. Marketing Calendar
2. Billboard
3. Flyers
4. Door to Door
5. Business Cards

A marketing calendar can help you keep track of what your business needs to be marketing, how your billboard ad should be advertising, what your flyers and social media posts should say, who should get a business card, and what doors and neighborhoods you should be sending your flyer to. A marketing calendar can help with the flow of your new clients and past clients. I use a marketing calendar in my childcare to help with what I am marketing for that month so my focus will only be on that. For example, for my pre-K program, I started marketing in February to my email list, then in March I started marketing to the community. I have my flyers done for the month and my phones ready to receive the calls for now enrolling in our pre-K program, ages three to five years of age.

Billboard statistics show from a study that 71% of Americans consciously look at billboard messages while driving. Thirty-seven percent report looking at an outdoor ad each or most of the time they pass one, 26% noted a phone number written on a billboard, and 28% noted a website address written on a billboard (Harleydream.org). Billboards can show off your business logo, colors, and website, and offer a gift. My billboard ad has generated over 75 new enrollments to have us broadcast on radio stations in Cleveland, TN. Stop by your billboard and go live a few times a week till you have enough people calling asking about your services. What all should you have on your billboard? Your location, phone number, free offer, logo, hours of operations, website, and age of your program.

Flyers are also good to pass out within your community and when you are out in your local grocery stores and at appointments. When you see a bulletin board, post one of your flyers on one with the tear tags to give you a call. Flyers can make your business visible to people who do not know your business. I always make my flyers match my brand and have my logo branded on the flyer. I got this tip from my coach to add some parents and their testimonies onto your flyers as well. I have placed my now enrolling flyers onto Facebook ads, and I have had success with parents from going to my website and filling out a pre-enrollment form to touring to full enrollment.

Door to door still works. Getting a company to make you some small postcards and have them mailed out to one hundred fifty to three hundred family houses can get your phones ringing with enrollments. I went to my local post office and asked if I could mail to the area codes of a certain area, and the price was low to where I enrolled 13 kids off 25 postcards. I had a few people call and some drive by, and I still would give them brochures about my business. When they see me at a local event, they remember getting a postcard from Tiny Tigers, and the enrollment process begins.

Below, write down some marketing ideas that you would want to start doing in your business and start taking Fast Action.

_____

_____

_____

_____

How to go from twenty-eight to staying open late.

Now listen, from twenty-eight to staying open late, here is my outcome. I was able to achieve full enrollment with two different shifts, fully staffed. Paying my rent on time and paying for a coach and getting the training, to owning my own curriculum, The Educational Learning Express. Go scan the barcode below, I have a free offer. From being nominated two times in a row for best childcare in Chattanooga, TN, to being voted for *"Who's Who Of America Business "* 2021. From creating an outstanding website to having my childcare center commercials and billboards around the city of Chattanooga. I set up tours on the weekends when my business could've been closed. I have former customers that used to attend my program that still send referrals my way. I hired a bookkeeper, a CPA, and childcare coach to help sustain my childcare business. Making partnerships with my chambers of commerce and Early Matters, T-Mobile, Helan Healthcare, and serving on the housing board has strengthened my business. From having a great relationship with my landlord, which helped me with my past-due rent, building my enrollment, to building my staff, I set some methods in place to keep our enrollment from getting low ever again.

In my research, I have found that these strategies have helped other successful business owners keep track of their clientele. I have walked you through the 7 Millionaire Strategies that have helped me turn my enrollment around in 30 days. Go grab your favorite journal, your pen, and let's go.

I hope that you took great notes and I have helped explain how you can go from low enrollment and come back with full enrollment by using millionaire secrets and working your business till you have a waiting list. I have learned to never give up and to keep focusing on my business and to trust the process. Let's go and increase your enrollment in 30 days. Don't forget your free gift . Scan the barcode below

ABOUT THE AUTHOR

My name is LaShon Carter. I was born and raised in Chatta-nooga, TN as my mom's only child and one of seven on my dad's side. My parents wanted to provide the best education for us, so they sent us to schools that were not in our home district. With the additional bus stops and the distance, this means it took 2 hours or more to get to school. This also means my school days were 4 hours longer than my friends and classmates. I graduated from Ooltewah high school (C/O 2006); I then went on to Chattanooga State Technical Community College. From there I received a degree in Human Services, which is 1 of many degrees that I have. I still currently attend school to further my education in the Childcare field.

I started loving teaching at a young age. I remember around seven playing school with my dolls, bears and sometimes my imaginary friends. I would set myself aside on the side of the room which I shared with my two sisters and one brother and I would set it up like a classroom. I assigned my inanimate students' homework, teaching my imaginary students how to add/subtract, and created lessons for writing and reading. My dad was the principal, and my mom was the vice principal, I remember this like yesterday. I would sometimes take control of the bathrooms for hours reading and writing inside the bathrooms just teaching myself how to add subtract and doing fun cool science projects. I remember in middle school having trouble with English in math and as silly as it sounds, I went back to teaching my imaginary class. I passed my English and math test when I went back to teaching my imaginary students laugh out loud. I loved playing sports in middle school so in order to continue playing sports I had to keep my grades up. I love playing basketball, soccer, and volleyball, but my favorite sport was track & field. My track coach at Hunter middle school will always remind me how hard I worked and that my work ethic was better than my peers. What I really wanted to tell my coach is that my parents were crazy, and I was afraid to let them down. Therefore, every day on the bus ride home I would work on my system of making sure that I had better grades, I would work on my reading assignments, writing, science assignments and I would do it on the bus with my imaginary class.

Fast forward a little to when I spent 6 years working for a child-care provider. I enjoyed so many different aspects of my class from helping the parents understand the importance of breast-feeding, watching the little ones grow all my infant parents loved me watching over their little ones, one of my parents I continued to keep in touch with to this day, always reminds me that her child was showed so much love and was taught so much under my care. After being in the infant room for over 4 years I moved up to assistant director with no formal training at all. To help me understand and adapt to the new role, I spent a good bit of time learning what I could off the clock. I created a binding system for that company, which they still use to this day. I understood God put me here for a reason. When I left this job, I lost my passion for children. I changed jobs a few times and I finally thought I found a job I would love and stick with for a while, being a sales merchandise. I had 13 stores I would have to go to and all I could talk about was saving money to invest into my own childcare business. I will never forget my last day working there. I went to work with a pain in my side and I immediately scheduled a doctor's appointment. The doc-tor scheduled a CT scan to look at what was going on inside my body after getting the bad news that my hernias had returned but this time it was three massive hernias that could kill me if I continue working the job. I looked at my husband with tears wondering what we will do for funds and have two kids to raise and bills that were piling up. Three days after being home a knock at my door one of my parents from a job I left a long time ago asked me to watch her two beautiful children. And my home daycare journey begins when my love for children returns. My daughter and two other students started Tiny Tigers Family home daycare three kids turned into seven kids, seven kids turned into 24 and before I knew it, we were growing. I opened Tiny Tigers Learning Center in 2017 with eight kids and ended up with 50 before my 30 days of being open.

Tiny Tigers Learning Center has been nominated two times in a row for best daycare in Chattanooga TN and we serve on three different boards that help support early education. We have opened a new business titled The Educational Learning Express, where we are making education fun. After you make your first purchase, please enjoy your free gift when you enter this code at checkout "learn2021". I enjoy teaching other educators how to bring fun back into their classroom programs changing the way we think about education making it more enjoyable for the students and the educators. We are launching our new program here in the spring which is called The Educational Corner where we consult parents and teachers with their educational needs. With helping with classroom management tips with lesson plans, free newsletters and assessments tools to help with their child or children..

Go online today letsgoexpress.org and set up your consultant services. Use the code **TeachMe** at checkout to get a discount.

Special thanks

To my wonderful and supportive husband L.C. Carter for supporting me over the years we won some and lost some, but through it all you never stop believing in me. I want to thank you for loving me and encouraging me to go for what I love. You have done so much for our family and I love you and I am so excited for what is in store for us.

To my children Jashawn and La'Mya you continue to push me to become a better mother. Thank you for sharing me with the world. I thank you for always helping me even when you could be playing your video games. You take time to support your mother. Continue to use wisdom and guidance throughout life. I love you and mama will always support you.

To my parents, sister and brothers, thank you for your support and dealing with my messy room at times and being hard on me when I need it. I love you and thank you again for your support.

To my family and friends and Tiny Tigers Staff I love you all and thank you for your support.

LaShon Carter
"With God all things are Possible" Luke 1:37

PARENT AND CHILDREN RETENTION

THE DAY TACO BELL
CHANGED MY LIFE

Sometimes we make choices and sometimes our choices are divinely aligned for us. I'm going to share my journey and a pivotal moment at Taco Bell that would change my life forever.

I walked into Taco Bell one winter day, as a mother and paralegal who mediated family matters and advocated for children, and I left with a tremendous burden on my heart. That day, as my then 7-year-old daughter and I enjoyed each other's company, laughing and joking, there was another young girl about my daughter's age experiencing quite a different encounter. This child sat with her red face hung low as her mother totally humiliated her and spoke to her as though she were less than a human. My heart broke. I remembered thinking to myself, there is so much love in the world and it's free, yet still, there are children who go through their childhood unable to identify with this feeling of unconditional love. At this, I decided to open my home up to foster children and share the abundance of love that filled my household. Children that had previously been written off with no hope of getting any better, thrived in my care. My keenness to support my daughter's learning grew and I knew I needed a shift. Advocating for children in family matters no longer seemed enough and fulfilling for me. It was time to shift my practice to the direction of an early childhood educator.

I left my position as a rising paralegal and began a position as an early childhood assistant. After being at that company for just under two years, the time had come for me to get my certification. I was always thankful for the leadership of my then supervisor, Karen Grant, and her acknowledgement and support of my calling, talents, and giftings. As my co-workers and I celebrated on that last day, I was humbled to hear a group of ladies who I looked to and admired share that they also looked to me and appreciated and emulated my strategies and positivity with the children. Fast forward to my completion of the program, holding various positions in the field, I am now an assistant early childhood educator at one of the most coveted companies, set to work my way up. I experienced a similar favor at this position. The Center Quality assurance rater wanted to know who I was. She was very impressed with my work, saying, *"if it wasn't for me, they would not have scored an almost perfect rating."* A supervisor was confused about how they'd fallen out of the loop and not knowing that the center had a new supervisor. Though the word supervisor never came out of my mouth, there was something all over me.

Things had taken a sharp turn. Racism, neglect, abuse, and disgruntled employees surfaced. What's worse is the embedded mechanism used to cleverly disguise. Being newer with a heart for service and a desire to do my part in children's and families' lives, to stand up and stand out for their rights, my eyes were opened. When I spoke out, I was demoted in my position under the guise of operational needs, and my hours were slashed in half. I had a strong sense of disbelief and my faith in the system was dwindling. Child Protective Services, supervisors, program manager, and program director all refused to take action by handing it off to another. I was doing my part, why wasn't anyone else? Who will protect the children or even the staff?

It's all coming together now. God had ordered my steps and brought me to this place at this time. Childhood memories of my mom and her mentor as she set her home daycare up, memories of researching how to start a school that the children would come out with superior moral character and godly excellence. Memories of all the classes and workshops I took about childhood development as my daughter grew, memories of all the daycare and school meetings I was always asked specifically to weigh in on, memories of parents always feeling comfortable with their children coming to our house when it was a hard no to anyone else, memories of foster parenting, memories while going to school of wanting more than to simply work on the floor as an educator in someone else's daycare; I have a style, a philosophy that builds on strengths. What leaders of this organization may have meant for evil by continuously throwing me into some of the most unique and challenging staff, parent, and child dynamics was for my good. It was my playing field to test and perfect my philosophy. My reputation precedes me—both staff and supervisors expected results and I delivered.

My choice was aligned for me, predestined, and this was my time to shine. What a moment in my story, that day at Taco Bell.

I want to talk to you about some of my methods and strategies that have enabled me to continue in my field happily and joyfully, that have kept generations returning for the Sparrow Kidz experience. I have word-of-mouth, referrals and loyal parents who bring back their second and third child. I have brought employees and grandchildren into my care from their experience, the strategies that have caused parents to drive 45 minutes across the city just to have their child in my care. Make no mistake, parents can see how we are caring for their children. They can see how clean we're keeping them, what we're feeding their intellect, what we're feeding them socially, physically, and what we are feeding into their souls. If we are in the childcare business and not doing right by the children, then we have no childcare business and we have no business being in the childcare business, PERIOD!

When we think of advocating for children, our first thoughts may be of abuse, neglect, and trafficking, or even lobbying for girls to have equal opportunities in other countries; something that demands a call to justice, if you will… While these are all true, there are other forms of child advocacy that play out on a day-to-day basis in less obvious forms. I would like to introduce the concept of effective child advocacy beginning with a child's core circle; the child themself, educators, and parents.

I will be sharing the **"Sparrow Kidz" Method** that produced the above results by examining:

1) edifying children in communication as a form of advocacy,
2) being/cultivating reflective educators as a form of advocacy, and lastly,
3) incorporating such advocacy into your program.

1. Speak Up to Your Kids

With so much negativity and bustling in the world, it has become humans' default to point out what's wrong over what is good and right. Praising, uplifting, and complementing is not natural but a form of communication to be mindfully practiced. If we are to continuously feed the good, right, and positive, then eventually, the less desirable will fall away and be overtaken by the good. Self-fulfilling prophecy is the process through which an originally false expectation leads to its own confirmation. In a self-fulfilling prophecy an individual's expectations about another person or entity eventually result in the other person or entity acting in ways that confirm the expectations," as defined by Britannica, and it works both ways. It all starts with a child's actions; our response at this moment is critical. From the child's actions will stem our beliefs, the child's subsequent actions, our beliefs, and back to the child's actions again; it is the beginning of a cycle. If a child knows an adult/educator sees them as trouble, they are always being told they are bad and always encountering consequences for this bad behavior, then what is the incentive to do better? Likewise, if a child is consistently hearing what is good about them, it is less likely they will seek attention from engaging in bad behavior or have the opportunity and desire to and will also be easier to handle when a concern or correction is addressed lovingly and honestly. Just as easily as we can give children something to live down to, we can give them something great to aspire to.

So, what does this look like practically?

1) Say what you want instead of what you don't want.
2) Address the behavior and consequences instead of the child. (The child's behavior may have been bad, but they are not bad.)
3) Frequent and genuine praise that is specific and age appropriate. (The child knows what they are being praised for and it is a meaningful accomplishment for their developmental level.)

2. HOT Intelligence at Work

As the old proverb says, "give a man a fish and he eats for a day, teach him to fish, he eats for a lifetime." Hold that thought in mind as we dive further in. One of the best and most effective ways to uplift a child as a form of advocacy is to frame their thinking in such a way that supports healthy brain architecture, a sense of self-worth and an ability to critically think, process, and respond. Years ago, Harvard University released a study concluding that though children in this generation demonstrate great test performance, they lack critical thinking skills. The necessity of cultivating the next generation to feel, think, process, and respond in a positive manner is so needed now in our time and society.

What happens when a child totally and utterly flips out because the seam of their socks is irritating them, or because a child took their small red truck, meanwhile there are three other small red trucks that are identical? Being a toddler or a preschooler with a limited view of the world can be a bit egocentric. It is a seemingly small concern of no consequence to an adult but the world to a child. This scenario can go one of two ways: they are able to self-regulate with or without assistance, or they are not able to and spiral into an overwhelming mix of emotions. I've often used what seems to be an exaggerated example but, if our co-worker was crying or feeling down about their deceased or separated partner, would you respond to them by saying, "it was only…," "it's already been three years," "why don't you just," or "you should just move on"? In the same way this would be a big deal to your co-worker, what may seem trivial to you can be a big deal to children. With this in mind, it is important to meet the children where they are without judging the thing. Understand them on their level and allow them to feel their feelings and then to express them.

So, what does this look like practically? The formula I created and currently use at my center and in training is called A.V.A.R which stands for Acknowledge, Validate, Assist & Reassure.

A- Acknowledge the situation and that the child is experiencing intense emotions and help them to identify the emotion. For example, "I see that you're crying, are you sad, upset, disappointed, frustrated?"

V-Validate their feelings without bias. You could say, "I understand you being frustrated because you're having a hard time doing XYZ."

A- Assist in problem solving by prompting such open-ended questions as, "what would you like to happen?" "what do you need?"' "what can you do about it?" Listen, engage, and respond intently.

R- Reassure the child that they and/or it will be okay by reminding them of similar past experiences or directing them to the hope and potential of the future.

3. Challenge Nos and Can'ts

Challenge your nos! We know that children cannot always have what they want and need to be able to problem solve, self-regulate, and maneuver those conversations and/or events. That being said, challenge your nos! Evaluate how and when we're using the word no. Picture with me a beautiful, lush forest or garden, with a specific path that is walked through multiple times a day. Eventually, that path gets broken in, and among that lustrous garden there's one pathway that is just soil, dirt, or gravel. That pathway has been trodden down and it's visible to any passer-by that this is the route to get from point A to B. Now, picture this as the brain frequently hearing the word no. What messages are associated with this word? Negativity, it's wrong. I can't. I should stop. I shouldn't try…. On average, by the time a child is 17 years old, they've heard the word no 150,000 times and have only heard the word yes 5,000 times. What pathways in the brain have been created, what is dominating? So, what do we say to support the architecture of a strong and healthy brain?

So, what does this look like practically?
Replace "Nos" with:

1) What you want/redirect or inform.
Instead of saying "no hitting" say and demonstrate "gentle touches," "hands are for…," "use your word to express yourself."

2) What the situation is.
Instead of saying, "no, we can't go outside today," you might say, "it is -20 degrees today and we would turn into human icicles if we went to play at the park today."

3) Yes with a condition.

Instead of saying, "no, you can't watch TV," try "yes, you can watch tv after you clean your room."

The word "Can't" can become a limiting word that sends the mind into self-defeat. At my family learning and play center, the words "I can't" are bad words. I teach my children to replace "I can't" with, "I will", "I need", "I need more help", "I need more time","I need to practice a little more," or whatever it is that they need.

4. The Reflective Educator

Educate comes from the root word educare; to rear up, nurture, to draw out, and to extrapolate. If there is something that can be pulled out, that means there's capacity, for every child to learn, to grow, to develop, and to go and be amazing. This also means that as educators and childcare center owners, we have a duty to not just run a program but to powerfully plant seeds in our children's lives and train them up well in all spheres of their lives to walk in and pursue their awesomeness.

Staff reflection of themselves and of children is key when it comes to edifying children. When I designed my program, I designed it with this in mind and made sure that there was time built into the program so that staff would be able to reflect. This can be done before school, after school, during naptime, when you're planning your curriculum, at staff meetings, or whenever else it can be fit in. It's important for staff to reflect on their practices, their biases, and the children. We need to be able to see ourselves as powerful educators planting seeds, and understand that we are constantly being watched and whether we like it or not, whether we signed up for it or not, we are role models. These children spend more of their waking time with us than they do perhaps their own families.

So, what does this look like practically?

Grab a pen and write below the answers to the questions as educators and childcare center owners.

1) How do you see yourself?
2) What is the legacy that you want to leave behind?
3) What is your why, why are you here?
4) What are your gifts, your talents, your desires that bring you here at this time for this purpose?

_____

_____

_____

_____

_____

_____

_____

_____

_____

_____

_____

_____

At my center, I have my staff reflect on the children once a week. Every Monday morning before we start work, we write all the children's names down and at least five positive attributes about each child, and we think about what they could be and what we would like to see for them in the future. If we see our children in high esteem, if we see them as the precious gems that parents are entrusting us with, if we see them as God's masterpiece, this begins to frame our interactions with them and it becomes natural for us to build them up and for us to speak up to them.

My last point is perhaps the most obvious, but I would like to briefly touch on it. Every child is different. Recognizing and understanding children's gifts, personalities, adjusting your strategies to suit them and helping parents do the same gives parents an understanding and children a sense of self and belonging. The techniques and forms of communication you may use for an outgoing and decisive child may not be effective for a cautiously quiet child. It is important to know your children and their personalities and to be able to plan curriculum and environmental, verbal, and behavioral strategies around this. Never compare children, let them be their own selves and provide space and opportunities for them to be.

I would love to work with you on a one-on-one basis within my program called "Sparrow Kidz Services." We will focus on growth and development from the inside out. My mission is to **"Empower to Succeed" one person and one child at a time.** Let's connect at: www.sparrowkidzservices.com

ABOUT THE AUTHOR

Maureen Ramnath is a Registered Early Childhood Educator, Child Advocate, Founder and CEO of Sparrow Kidz Services. Maureen embodies a strong conviction to empower children and families to succeed through the building of children's healthy identity, extracting strengths she positions children for a lifetime of success.

Maureen has created Rising Stars and Big Promises curriculum, parent and educator coaching programs as well as learning solutions which include, private in home, family play and learn center and online learning opportunities. Maureen specializes in strength-based curriculum, educating parents and educators as well as positive behaviour guidance and growth.

This forward thinking professional has taught over 170 children and worked with over 100 families in her over 15 years of experience. Maureen Ramnath has worked collaboratively with the Family Resources Program, Toronto Public Health.

She has also been instrumental in revising effective childcare policies for one of the largest childcare institutions in Toronto, ON. Over her career she has also held supervisory, consulting and lead teaching positions. Maureen Ramnath has been an active community leader, youth engagement worker and foster parent.

Maureen is tremendously thankful and blessed to be mother to a brilliant, multifaceted young woman and grandmother to a wise, funny and high-spirited young girl. Maureen Ramnath began Sparrow Kidz Services in 2008 as an afternoon school program, within the first three months the program had a waitlist and Maureen watched her children soar as every student rose by one grade level through the implementation of her philosophy and strategies. This visible growth prompted teachers to inquire of Maureen Ramnath's strategies and philosophies; which prepared the possibility to share her philosophy that would later be implemented in the classrooms.

Maureen continued outside employment as she grew her childcare and international consulting firm before transitioning to full time. Some of her students have returned to volunteer in the program for the high school credits, gone to be a successful nursing student, physiotherapist, medical administrations, law clerks, makeup artist, cosmetic mixologist, fashion stylist, entrepreneurs and have graduated with honours.

Students and grandparents have also returned to enroll their children for a second generation of the Sparrow Kidz experience.

For more information, please visit
www.Sparrowkidzservices.com

PARENT RETENTION "THE SERVE WELL CONCEPT METHOD"

NINE OUT OF TEN

Before we begin, I want you to think about this question and try to answer it. How many opportunities have you missed to increase enrollment in your child care business? I want you to take the time to write your answer below.

_____

_____

_____

_____

Now, I want you to get comfortable while I share a story with you about an experience that set me in motion to master a necessary skill to gain and retain the clients that add value to my business. You know, the Preferred Clients, because numbers in business only matter if they multiply.

By the end of this chapter, my goal for you is that you would understand this simple truth: "Money can't take you where your Character can't keep you."

Let me explain a bit.

In the year 2002, I had taken a job as center director at a child care establishment across town. This was actually my first experience in a management position at a child care facility. Up until then, I had always served as a lead preschool teacher, which I loved. The management experience I had prior to owning and operating my future child care business, not until 2006, was during the six years I worked in banking.

Even though customer service is engrained in every fiber of my being, I would soon learn that this experience would be my introduction into the importance of "serving" and valuing child care clients.

The incident that I'm preparing to share with you was nothing short of a recipe for disaster. The components included a flustered parent and a child care worker with total disregard to meeting the needs of this parent. As you may know, a day in child care is filled with transitions. The most important being arrival and departure. These two are critical because they provide many opportunities to extend exceptional customer service to clients. It's important for you to understand that these "opportunities" or interactions equate to making a deposit into your bank account. While it's true that we serve several other groups in child care, I want to focus on The Client group during this chapter.

Serving requires one to "observe" and "pay close attention" to the spoken and unspoken needs of others. Did you know that almost 96% of customers say customer service is important in their choice of loyalty to a brand? (Forbes.com). Let's take a moment to allow this information to sink in. Here is what I heard, nearly 100% of the customers surveyed want business owners, you and I, to know that the treatment they receive will either cause our businesses to experience multiplication or on the contrary, experience lack. Wow! If you hadn't already, are you now beginning to understand the critical role of serving in your business?

A client who shows up every day is not an example of loyalty. Remember, when it comes to business, multiplication is important. In other words, if that client that shows up every day is not converting into new money, either through upscaling or recruiting new clients, they should not be considered reliable. Here's another example. As a Dominion Energy customer, I pay my bill each month without incident. Why? Because I have grown accustomed to my dark rooms becoming illuminated by light at the flip of a switch. This necessary expense is factored into my budget. However, as their customer, I have not been wowed to the point that I would promote their services to anyone else. All they should expect to get from me is the payment for the energy I have used. And not only that, the second a competitor comes along to promote an energy service that is a better fit for my needs, I would switch without hesitation. Again, showing up does not mean that your client is loyal to your business.

Now, back to this incident that caused me to pivot. It occurred during departure one evening. Parents were arriving to pick up their children back-to-back, like any other day. Have you ever really observed the look and posture of the parents as they arrive for pickup? I'm sure, just like me, you notice that many of them appear tired after a day of working. Similar to the way child care providers typically feel at the end of the day. When parents arrive, they generally just want to pick up their little ones and head home to complete the next phase of the evening.

My office, at this center, was within sight of the front door. At one point, I observed a staff member open the door for a parent arriving to pick up a student. The staff member called for the student and when he came downstairs, he did not have his coat. The child's mother then looked at the staff member and said, "Do you know where his coat is?" to which the staff member replied, "I don't know," while shrugging her shoulders. The worst part was when the staff member walked away without assisting the parent any further. I will never forget the look of hopelessness and exhaustion on that mom's face. This staff member completely missed a golden opportunity to boost client loyalty, enhance the brand reputation of the business, present herself as a professional and source of support, or ease what appeared to be a pain point for this client. The lack of character and professionalism this staff member chose to display created a level of frustration with the client, which is a fast way to create a deficit in any business.

This parent didn't stay long and neither did I. The tone and execution of a successful customer service strategy must be initiated and demonstrated by those at the very top of the chain of command first. Everyone else serving under this rank will usually only rise to the level of expectation in demonstration. Unfortunately, the owners of this child care service did not provide training for or demonstrations of excellent customer service.

Nelson Mandela, who was known for his character and remarkable leadership abilities, once said, "**Vision** without **action** is just a dream, **action** without **vision** just passes the time, and **vision** with **action** can change the world."

Take a moment to really think about your vision. Are the words living? Are those words felt by your clients? Without seeing your written vision, I'm pretty confident that there is a promise to "serve well" in some capacity. How do you measure whether your business is living up to its promises?

You see, I don't recall whether this child care center previously mentioned operated with a vision or any kind of systems. This center is still in business today but continues to struggle with enrollment.

This was not a lost endeavor. I learned valuable information that would help me to do it better, or as my Coach says, "Build it bigger."

Fast forward several years from this experience. I have worked with countless child care providers who do not initially prioritize customer service in their businesses.

I need to pause for a moment to make sure you understand what I am teaching here. Customer service is not simply being nice and kind to your customers and clients. It's not saying "Oh, I love your jacket Mrs. Jones" or "How was your day?" And it's certainly not a department. There is a psychological method and science to providing extraordinary experiences for your customers and clients. It must take care and thought much in the same way when choosing a curriculum, screening candidates for employment, or preparing for a major marketing event. The great thing is that once you have created a master calendar for preplanned customer service experiences, you simply train your team from your calendar and follow it each year.

It's important that you shift your mind regarding customer service. Mastering customer service has allowed my businesses to experience multiple benefits over the years.

With my "Serve Well Concept" where we bring back the care in childcare, I teach over 26 concepts and methods that will help you and your staff gain and retain loyal clients. These concepts, along with others, keep me and my team on a consistent record of converting 9 out 10 tours into new clients. I'm going to share seven of those with you. So if you need to run and take a potty break, now is a good time. And don't forget to grab your note paper, highlighters, and pencils. I want you to be fully present without any distractions.

The seven concepts I am going to share with you are:

1) Believing in the organization you represent

Believing in the organization is vital to the operation and growth of the business you own or represent. The level of faith that you have in the business and its ability to impact lives will be visible in your day-to-day operations and interactions. Your belief in the business will be necessary during undesirable cycles or situations that business owners experience from time to time. There will be times you will need to draw strength from your original vision and motivation. This is not possible without first believing in your business. If you don't believe in your business, neither will your clients and staff.

2) Choose an attitude of service

The operative word here is "choose." We may not always feel like serving others. But it's important to remember that when we work in a service environment, like child care, we have made a commitment to focus on the needs of others. Whatever is going on in our day should never cause a negative impact to our customers. Your attitude can literally produce increase or lack in your business.

3) Find the pain points

Have you ever had to reach out to a business due to a problem? Or have you ever disconnected from a business or service due to consistent frustration? These were probably "pain points" for you. What annoys or frustrates your clients? When clients consistently experience frustration, it is not possible to expect them to be loyal to your brand. If you have never asked your clients about their frustrations, I urge you to do so. You don't want to be in the dark about this or worse yet, ignore it. Here is one way to begin. Offer a simple survey that focuses on the individual areas of your business. One example is to offer a tour survey after a prospective client tours your facility. This will give you insight as to what you may need to add or remove from that service. Your survey must be strategic, avoid questions like, "How did we do?" Visit our site for free training on using and understanding surveys.

4) Create self-serve options

Serving others is not a one-size fits all approach. Just as we all have different learning styles, we also need to consider the various needs of our customers when asking them to do business with us. I have found that more and more clients prefer handling much of their business online. Be sure to develop online options for registering, submitting paperwork, communicating, etc. This is an excellent option to present to clients because it assures them that they can handle some tasks outside of business hours, which may be more convenient for them.

5) Unexpected gestures

A successful customer experience will include many opportunities to wow your clients. Our clients tend to expect certain gestures such as sending a birthday card or sending flowers on Mother's Day. But consider the idea of exceeding expectations. Have you, as an example, sent a greeting card to the parents or other loved ones of your client? They don't do business with you but imagine the impression left by this gesture. What about mailing an unexpected activity kit addressed to the student. There are a plethora of creative ideas that will catch your clients off guard in a good way. I also recommend asking them to take pictures that you could use on your social media or in your marketing literature.

6) Verify satisfaction

As business owners or leaders, we find ourselves repeating information. If we are not careful, it can easily sound like a script. While I recommend using scripts, you want to avoid sounding like it. We must be aware that clients may need further explanation when we share information with them. Just because this information is familiar to us doesn't mean it's clear to the client. Whenever we communicate information to our clients, it's important for us to verify that they understand and are satisfied with the explanation. Keep in mind, our clients may not tell us if they understand. It's important to ask them. Use statements like, "Did that make sense?"; "Did I do a good job explaining this or what questions do you have"; "Does that answer your question?" The last thing you want is for a client to leave a conversation with you, without clarity.

7) Use a master customer experience calendar

Extending Customer Service and creating a Customer Experience Strategy does not come naturally to every business owner. Successful businesses depend on systems. For instance, if that little sticker in my car above my head was not present to remind me when I needed an oil change, I without doubt would end up driving a vehicle operating at less than peak performance. And it would probably continue until warning signs appear. Yet, this is how some of us operate our businesses. We do not prepare to avoid problems. Instead of being PROactive, we become Reactive. We end up putting out fires that we ourselves start by not meticulously planning. If this is you, I want you to know that you don't have to be the expert at everything in your business. It is, however, your responsibility to hire experts or invest in tools that will cause your business to thrive. I encourage you to take time to create a system for incorporating customer service and customer experiences into your business. This will prevent you and your team from guessing or wondering what your clients are thinking and if you and your team are doing enough to exceed their expectations. If you need help with this, I invite you to reach out.

In conclusion, these methods along with others created a pocket of ambassadors in my child care business. These are individuals who consistently promote my business and refer new clients. This caused me to create a Brand Ambassador program to reward those clients on another level. I know that these concepts and methods are proven to help businesses thrive in serving clients. Pick one concept and book your 15-minute session with me at **https://buildingchildcareprofessionals.com/p/free-15-min-success-call**and let's work together on your first concept. I look forward to serving as a guide and resource for you in the process.

ABOUT THE AUTHOR

Frances Davis is the founder of Serving Success in Child Care, a training and coaching consultancy specializing in equipping child care professionals to exceed expectations and experience overflow in their businesses with her "serve well" concept.

As a child care business owner and professional trainer and mentor with over 20 years in child care, she has seen how vital it is to prioritize the "Customer Experience" as it is a direct result of gain or loss in clientele. Hearing from other business owners about how her training and support helped to transform their staff and programs is one of her greatest accomplishments.

Some of her teachings and online courses include Behavior Management & Escalation, Phenomenal Phone Etiquette Training & Scripts, 12 Ways to Discipline Children for Early Child Care Professionals, and the highly requested Customer Service in Child Care course. She also offers a plethora of other management resources and tools to help child care businesses operate in excellence.

Frances also serves as a specialist on other national and international platforms in the childcare industry to include Jumpstart Bosses of America (member and Coach), The Council for Professional Recognition (PD Specialist), and ChildSavers (P.E.E.R. Mentor).

Frances lives in Richmond, VA with her husband and children.

If you would like to learn more or speak with Frances, feel free to visit www.servingsuccessinchildcare.com to schedule a free success call.

CHILD CARE
MARKETING AND
BRANDING STRATEGIES

DAYCARE DIVA MAINSTREAM MARKETING STRATEGIES

Can you build a brand so powerful and impactful that when you move, your enrolled families move with you? Picture this: you're given short notice and you must uproot your current enrolled families and find a new childcare location. You are not given an exact date, but you know the time is ticking. Each day you are receiving phone calls about the property you are renting going into foreclosure; the bank will own it. What will you do? Will you rent a house or buy a house, will you get a childcare center? How long will this process take? So many questions ran through my mind: how will I tell my parents?

What will my parents think? Will they relocate with me?

Welcome to New York, the home of the big apple. I am Lashanda Fraser, also known as the Daycare Diva. I started my childcare journey at the tender age of nineteen. I always had a passion and desire to teach children to dream big. I can remember growing up and playing school with my cousins. We had a principal, chef, and teachers. We had everything. I never realized just how much schools and teachers have in common with daycare. I grew up lining up my teddy bears to teach them.

I always thought I would be a teacher before I was introduced to the childcare industry. I was motivated and inspired by my mother and a childcare owner to start my very own daycare. I grew up hearing my mom say when she retired, she would open a daycare. So many ideas ran through my head of how I would decorate, how I would set up the daycare location. I wanted to create something powerful and meaningful. I started in a small apartment in Queens, New York. It took a mindset shift for me to realize my potential for many years. I told myself the apartment would not get approved. Who would approve of a daycare on the second floor of a three-story house? My mom and I were introduced to another childcare provider while providing transportation for her daycare; it was located in an even bigger building. I was in complete shock. Here was a licensed daycare on the fourth floor in a big building with an elevator. She encouraged us to go for it. She told me to step out on faith and everything will work out. Roy T. Bennett states, "You never change your life until you step out of your comfort zone; change begins at the end of your comfort zone."

That day, I made a decision that would change my life forever. I applied to open a family or group family child care program. I knew nothing about completing the application or where to start. I didn't know anything about how to run a business. I was a full-time student in college at that time, pursuing a teaching degree. I'm living proof that if you just start, start right now, start today, everything will fall into place. Guess what? The hard work paid off. I pushed and persevered, and my license was handed to me. To my surprise, I started to advertise my childcare program and the benefits that my program had to offer using my marketing skills at that time I didn't even know I had. I thought I was just promoting my business to get clients. I would pass out flyers, brochures, and I wore tee-shirts. I was a walking advertisement. My phone did not stop ringing with people interested in enrolling. I would set up an interview, and time after time, no one would come or very few people showed up. I never got discouraged. I studied and learned why people were not coming because they never knew the daycare was in an apartment. Due to how I was marketing and branding my program, they thought I was a high-quality center.

They didn't like the appearance or just figured I didn't have much to offer due to the daycare business being inside of the apartment. Boy, were they wrong it was the complete opposite. This caused me to speak greatness into my business. I changed my whole marketing and branding technique. I constantly advertise with flyers, I networked with different schools, crossing guards, and other businesses in my community. I advertised online and I created a website. This caused me to rethink my business. To my surprise, I began to grow quickly beyond my capacity. I had to create a waiting list. I created a brand for my childcare program and created a relationship within my community. I decided to pivot.

I decided to move to a nicer looking and bigger location. I extended my hours to accommodate the requests I was getting for nontraditional hours. When the doors first opened, two children were enrolled and that family referred another child. This was my introduction to referrals. When I decided to move locations, I was nervous since I was going to an unfamiliar area. I had already made a name for myself in Richmond Hill. My childcare program began to host events for children. My first daycare did not have the traditional look. This caused me to start marketing on another level. I had to work twice as hard to get families enrolled because many judged my program just from the appearance on the outside. This caused me to create a variety of flyers and to create a strong social media presence.

I started with Facebook. This caused me to think outside of the box with my marketing strategy. I created a ton of activities and events to grow my enrollment. I would constantly show how the kids were excelling and advancing academically and all the fun we had. This generated a waiting list that gave confirmation it was time to move. I moved and my parents moved too. This was the first time I learned the importance of being impactful. I knew I was providing quality care and helping families. I value parent engagement and creating a family-like atmosphere. "As you go about creating new customer engagement programs and direct marketing packages for your brand, look for opportunities to give rather than to get. Whoever makes the first kind gesture, as studies show, tends to gain the most." — Jeanette McMurtry.

My waiting list continued to grow at my new location. Children in my program were getting all A's, kids were being promoted to the next grade, and kids were socially growing. I created annual events. My daycare program became known for hosting a ton of events. My parents were engaged. Every year I would host a prom, graduation, and moving up ceremony just to name a few. I was doing things in my home program that other home child care programs were not doing. I created an experience like no other. I always felt I had to give more because people judged home programs as just "babysitting."

I changed that stigma with my high-quality program. I stayed at my second location for seven years. My daycare was always at capacity. My waiting list continued to grow and grow. Everything was going great until the day I got a knock at the door. I was used to people stopping by to get information. I proceeded to get the door with business cards and a brochure in hand.

"Hi, good afternoon, how can I help you?"

"Ma'am, I'm just here to let you know the bank will auction this home off soon."

"Excuse me, you must be mistaken. I pay my landlord every month."

"No ma'am, the bank will be contacting you, goodbye."

I had to move and move fast. I'd moved already, so I wasn't scared to move again. I just didn't know if I would have enough time. The day came and I typed up a letter to let my parents know that I would be moving locations. I invited everyone to the open house at the new location.

My parents didn't blink; they congratulated me on the move to another bigger location. I was no longer renting. I now owned the two-family home my daycare was located in. Everyone traveled with me. Wow! I was shocked that my parents were willing to uproot and travel to still attend my program. Some parents had to travel an additional 15-50 minutes just to get to the new location. Some families used to just walk to daycare, now they would have to commute. This happens when you build a strong relationship with your parents. I shouldn't have been shocked at all. I built a strong foundation over the years.

It's moving day and to my surprise, there are two other daycares located on my block. Can your business survive not only a move but also being located on the same block with two other programs? I didn't doubt myself or my program for one second. I did not fear the other daycares nor did I look at them as competition. Growth is a beautiful thing. It was at that very moment that I realized I created the system, the blueprint to help not only myself but other providers. I was sure in my abilities and the benefits my program had to offer, that I would continue to grow, and the right clients would come no matter where I moved or if I was located in between two other daycares. I knew that my community needed my service and everything I had to offer.

The open house party was great. Parents came, some brought gifts, some came to see the new location, alumni children and their parents came to support. My heart was overwhelmed. I believed in my daycare and I believed in my program so much and what we had to offer that I didn't fear change. See, something happens deep down on the inside of you. It's a feeling you can't escape when you know it's time to give your dreams all you got. "Learn to adapt. Things change, circumstances change. Adjust yourself and your efforts to what is presented to you so you can respond accordingly. Never see change as a threat, because it can be an opportunity to learn, to grow, evolve and become a better person." — Rodolfo Costa

The doorbell is ringing, the phones are ringing off the hook. Our Instagram page is full of DMs from prospective families who are interested in enrolling. One parent said, "Hey, I would love for my child to do all the cool stuff I see other children doing on your Instagram." Once again, a waiting list is created. I will never forget the day we hosted graduation. It was so different in 2020. I planned a graduation during COVID-19. I wanted to keep the legacy and the tradition of the daycare going. I did not want to cut the children and their parents from the experience. I pushed through and made the necessary adjustments to give the families and the children an experience they will remember for a lifetime. During the drive-by graduation, unbeknownst to me, another family was looking from around the corner. There is a schoolyard directly across from me, so you can see straight through the next block.

Would you believe that another family saw the quarantine theme graduation and was intrigued?

They watched the whole thing and on that same day, they wanted to enroll. They came over to introduce themselves to say "hi, I saw the whole graduation. I would love to sign my daughter up." Just from one event, I had a family ready to enroll and start right away. I have successfully learned to build a brand and a name for myself. I have moved my group family child care program three times, all while keeping families enrolled for over seven years. The families enrolled in my program stay with me. It is a pleasure watching their precious little ones grow up right in front of my eyes. It is an honor that I get to be a part of their lives. I constantly market even though I am at capacity. I always build my waiting list. Word of mouth has grown my program. I'm so thankful that my parents referred me to other parents all the time. I learned true marketing strategies that work.

Even during a pandemic, I am at full capacity. I branded and marketed my program in such a way that I can survive in any season. That's why I created Daycare Diva Consulting LLC to help inspire and uplift other providers or people who inspire to own and operate their very own daycare. I'm here to teach you techniques to win in your program with proven marketing and branding techniques. Daycare Diva Consulting LLC was created to help childcare providers put the pieces together to build their childcare empire. I can show you how to market and brand your home daycare or your childcare center. I show you how to provide quality no matter your location, big or small. I mastered the techniques of creating multiple streams of income in my business and I can teach you to do the same in your home-based or center-based location.

Are you ready to grow your enrollment? Are you ready to boost your parent engagement?

I want to share with you my seven easy marketing strategies for attracting clients. Sit down and write down what your ideal client looks like. Where do they work, how much money do they make? What kind of person would they be? Once you gather your list, you can start to plan out how you will attract that target audience. Learn your ideal clientele.

Step 1: Know your clientele. After you have completed your research, it's time to come up with the ways you want your program to be represented. What do you want to be known for?

When people hear of your program, what do they think of it? Once you know how you want to be viewed and who your ideal clientele is, you create a plan on how to get those parents enrolled.

Step 2: Create a social media presence. Even if your program is not open yet. You want to let people know that you are coming and what to expect. The power of social media in today's time is essential in helping build your business. I remember the day my daycare was featured on Melissa and Doug Instagram. My daycare constantly receives people interested in collaborating or sending us items so we can promote their business. I was able to get free books and tee shirts just because people loved the way I marketed my program. The same is possible for you. You have to meet clients where they are. Most of the families now enrolling are from a younger generation. Instagram, Facebook, and YouTube is a big thing for the younger generation. My parents love to see little snippets of our day via social media, especially our Instagram stories. They can share with family and friends all over the world. I have created a sense of belonging. Families DM the daycare all the time, that's my niece, that's my nephew, so excited to see the scholars through social media. They can follow along with us each day.

Step 3: Host events. You can choose to do big or small events. Whichever you choose, sit down and write your why. Why are you having this event? What kind of event will it be? Is your goal to increase enrollment? How will this event help? I host a ton of events annually, big and small. This gives my parents a way to stay connected and engaged. If you are now opening a daycare, host an open house. Do it more than once, do it virtually. My open house was catered by a chef, I had refreshments, music, and activities for children to do. In my eleven years of being a childcare provider, I hosted a ton of events. I remember having so many families come out. It was a surprise event. I didn't tell them what kind of event I just told them to show up at a certain time. Everyone came. We had food, music, and played games. I gave out gifts to each family. It was recorded and is on our youtube page. It is a memory that the families and I can watch over and over again.

If you don't know what kind of events to host and how it will attract parents, I wrote an e-book that gives you a list of events and theme days you can host each month. Did you know specific months have designated days? For example, national popcorn day or national doctors' day. In my e-book, I break it down for you month by month, so you never miss an event. *Grab your e-book today at www.daycaredivaconsulting.com

Step 4: Create a referral program. Parents often refer my program to others. This is something I'm truly honored to receive. Creating a reward program and offering different incentives was something I had to do to reward my clients that constantly thought highly of my program to refer it to other parents. What kind of incentives can you create? Again, this goes back to knowing your ideal clientele. What do they like? It can be a gift card, money off tuition, a trip to the spa, you name it. A token of appreciation goes a long way. A referral program is not just for parents enrolled, but for anyone who tells someone about your program. Don't limit yourself!

Step 5: Build community relationships and partnerships. I have supported local businesses in my area. I have attended numerous networking events and hosted my very own networking events. In return, through conversations and getting to know them as I would shop in their businesses often, I began to foster a relationship. Businesses began to refer others to my daycare. Schools began to refer to my daycare, neighbors, the crossing guards, paraprofessionals in the schools, and still do till this day. I'm thankful for every single one of them. I built genuine relationships.

Step 6: Stand out. What will make you unique, what will you specialize in? One of the things I wanted to be known for was hosting events and bringing families together. I grew up in a loving family and wanted the children to feel that in my program.

I have the pleasure of working alongside my grandmother, mother, sister, and cousins. We have a special bond and I also share that with the kids enrolled in my program. How will you make your program stand out? We have many enrichment programs to help children be well-rounded and have exposure to a wide variety of things. What will make your program different?

I also wanted to be known for helping children blossom into scholars. So many children were graduating from my program and exceeding expectations in school. Scholars were reading. Most of the children stayed until preschool or kindergarten. Teachers would call and say that they are impressed with students who came from my daycare that are in their class. They know all their letters, sounds, colors, shapes, numbers, manners, you name it. I stood out because not only were we having fun with events, the kids were learning. I create interactive learning binders for my daycare to help children learn in a fun way. I make them unique and branded with my logo. I have learned how to teach children in a fun and creative way. I create my own curriculum and teach daycare owners to do the same in their programs. I would love to create your interactive learning binders for your childcare. Visit our website at www.daycaredivaconsulting.com

Step 7: Brand your childcare program. Many people have stated to me that my program looks like a private school.

I evolved over the years. I'm from the childcare provider era where we wore scrubs, but now my staff has uniforms. We have converted over to polo-style shirts. The children and staff have uniforms. We show our school pride through our branding. We have apparel, merch, workbooks, cups, patches, you name it, we have it all. Branding is one of the most important parts of building your business. It will tell parents what they can expect from you and differentiate you from other businesses. "Your brand is what other people say about you when you're not in the room." – Jeff Bezos, Amazon CEO. What will your daycare stand for? Tell that story through your brand. Put yourself in the mind of the parents you want to attract. What are they looking for in a daycare and how can you tell your story through your brand?

You have the tools you need to succeed. When I first started, I had to learn everything on my own. You don't have to do that now. You don't have to make the same mistakes I made. Success is knocking at your door. It's time to open it and let it in! Speak life into your business daily. When you have the right tools, it is easy to market like a franchise. I would love to assist you beyond this book. Let's get connected by visiting my website at www.daycaredivaconsulting.com

ABOUT THE AUTHOR

Childcare Entrepreneur, Childcare Consultant, Mentor, Event Planner, Author

Since her early childhood years Lashanda had a passion for teaching and inspiring children. Growing up in a Caribbean Guyanese household Lashanda also enjoyed hosting and planning parties as a sign of celebration.

Lashanda Fraser is the C.E.O of Marcy Precious Little 1's Daycare and Daycare Diva Consulting. Lashanda is also the founder of Sophisticated Women and Conversation which is a networking group where she has connected with women entrepreneurs in all fields.

Lashanda specializes in helping childcare providers or those as-piring to put the pieces together to build their childcare pro-gram. Lashanda teaches childcare providers how to brand and market their childcare program no matter the size while increas-ing parent engagement through proven strategies. Lashanda also teaches childcare providers how to host big and small events in their program to boost enrollment.

While attending college Lashanda was inspired to open Marcy Precious little 1's. Marcy Precious Little 1's is created off of a family environment of love. Growing up in a loving family Lashanda wanted to share that love with the children and fam-ilies enrolled in the program.

Marcy Precious Little 1's Daycare has grown over the years and helps inspire kids to reach their highest potential. Many chil-dren have been promoted to the next grade, received straight A's and 4's in school. Marcy Precious Little 1s is known for de-veloping a unique style of teaching with our interactive learning binders and workbooks. Lashanda also created custom interac-tive learning binders for other childcare programs.

Through 11 years of being a childcare provider, Lashanda has hosted a ton of events small and big bringing together the chil-dren and families in the program and community.

Graduations and moving up ceremonies, proms, family day and virtual events due to COVID-19. Each month you're guar-anteed to see events at her childcare program. Lashanda is the author of the E-book "Theme Day Event List". It's an ebook that you need for success in planning any events in your daycare. This guide also helps childcare providers host and pre-plan events in their program for boosting their enrollment.

Lashanda is on a mission to help bring awareness and change the narrative of home childcare providers and all daycare providers. Lashanda wants to inspire all providers no matter the size of your program or where your program is located you can provide quality care.

Networking is something Lashanda loves to do. So, let's connect.

To my loving family on both my mom and dad side Fraser/Forde thank you for the support and always believing in me I love you guys.

To my best friends and my support team I'm so blessed to have friends that ride for me, and encourage me. I love you guys to the moon and back.

To Marcy Precious Little 1's Daycare parents, and alumni, thank you for all your support throughout the years. I am forever grateful for all of you.

To my friends and everyone that has supported me along this journey, you are appreciated.

To all entrepreneurs no matter where you are in your journey, know that the life you dream for yourself is possible. You were made to do impossible things, believe in yourself and give it all you got!

Love always

Lashanda, The Daycare Diva

Let's connect! I would love to inspire, motivate and connect with you.

Contact Information:

Lashanda Fraser

email daycaredivaconsulting@gmail.com

www.daycaredivaconsulting.com

Instagram @Thedaycarediva

Follow my business instagram page @Marcypreciouslittle1sdaycare

Facebook @Lashanda DaycareDiva Fraser

Subscribe to my Youtube channel @Daycare Diva TV Lashanda, The Daycare Diva

Follow along the scholars journey on youtube @ Marcy Precious Little 1s Daycare

STAFF TRAINING AND RETENTION METHOD

STYLE: STANDARDS THAT YIELD LEARNING EXCELLENCE

If you want to train your staff to grind, then it's professional development action plan time!

Some of us were born with the grind and for others, it had to be sold separately. Merriam-Webster defines grind as one who works or studies excessively. I like to say I was born with an extra portion of grind. This innate sense of grind has enabled me to become the Childcare Enthusiast I am today. Learn how I went from diapers to destiny in childcare by taking one professional development training at a time.

My first experience working in a child care setting was as a teen at Tuny Haven Early Learning Center, which was located in downtown Philadelphia. I used to love telling my friends I worked in Center City. In exchange for my services, I would go on trips with the children, get my nails done, or go to the "Gallery" with my aunt on our breaks to shop. At Tuny, I learned how to engage with children, and interact with adults in a professional environment. Tuny Haven introduced me to professional development training in childcare. Gaining knowledge to perfect my skill set at a young age was indispensable. I was eventually hired as an employee at Tuny but would soon leave to work with my aunt at Children of Promise.

I started off making $5.75 an hour working at Children of Promise. Actually, it was probably less than that. Listen, I was just happy to have a job, eager to learn, and willing to work. I worked every position in that childcare from aide, camp counselor, to teacher in every age group, and special projects manager. My aunt considered me her eyes and ears on the floor, or the classroom as some might say. I was her assistant director in that childcare for 10 years before the pastor decided to close the facility.

That's when my aunt felt like it was a move of God to open her own center, and it was a no-brainer for me to join her. She had groomed me for this moment, or so she thought. She was the one who pushed me to go to different professional development training sessions. I conducted conferences with her. She signed for my early childhood education college classes to be paid for by TEACH. She was also the one who told me even if I was in school for an associates degree, I had to get a Child Development Associate credential (CDA) to be eligible for the $600 bonus from the Quality Rating Grant Program we participated in.

I was instrumental in assisting my aunt in opening her first child care center; it was six months of grind. Stepping into the role of director while being married, raising a family, operating a 24-hour childcare, and attending professional development on how to manage childcare was all training ground for me. My aunt had passed me the mantle, but it wasn't for me to carry it out at her childcare center.

After God released me from my aunt's child care in 2009, I went on to direct at a large facility in North Philadelphia. This was my first time on salary. I thought my $35,000 a year was doing something. What I didn't know was that the crooked path I was on was about to be made straight. Do you believe in coincidence? Well, I don't. I believe in Destiny. I believe that when you are faithful in the little things, God will give you more. I'll let you decide if the next step of my journey was coincidence, or destiny.

You see, my oldest child started child care when she was six months old. That's right, I didn't enroll her at the child care center where I worked. We needed our space. I enjoyed the child care center where my baby went. The childcare center and I had the same core values, they fed the children home-cooked meals, and their academic program was refreshing. It was owned by a no-nonsense older woman. She treated my first child well, so naturally, when I had two more children, they went to her too. This childcare center along with the owner literally watched me develop into the woman I am today. I can remember her being around when my husband and I married, when we purchased our first home, through advancement in our careers, when my oldest went to school, and the support she gave during our youngest child's sickle cell crisis. Her childcare center was ultimately a place of stability for my family and me. Essentially, I should not have been surprised about what happened in 2010.

In December of 2010, the owner of the childcare center where my children attended had decided to close due to her husband's death. Guess who she approached first! Me, of course! I was so shocked when she said she admired my grind, she watched my growth over the years, and that I reminded her of herself. I couldn't believe that she wanted to mastermind with my husband and I about starting our own childcare in her building. I still remember my husband saying "I have seen what you have done for others, now it is time for you to do that same thing for yours." God opened the door for my family to have our own child care center with everything we needed to get started. Well, do you believe that was coincidental, or was it destiny? I think only God could have orchestrated a blessing that big for little ole me.

We have been owning and operating our child care center for the last 10 years. You see, I have worked excessively, I have studied vigorously starting with a CDA and finishing with a master's degree in early childhood education so that you could learn expert secrets from a teacher that turned into a childcare boss!

At every level, I desired to exemplify and employ teachers that had **STYLE: Standards That Yield Learning Excellence**. If you do not hold your teachers, staff, or employees to a standard, how do you expect them to work your dream? They don't, you will endure high turnover, running a one-woman show, all while your hair is falling out. Because I went through the process of taking professional development training, and obtaining the CDA, I knew the formula. As long as I have a willing and able body, I can train them to be the best teacher, and so can you.

As the program manager, you are responsible for the successful delivery of that child care program. I achieved success by duplicating myself through my professional development plan. Professional development training refers to all training, certification, and education that an employee needs to excel in his or her career. The goal of the professional development training is to keep up to date with trends in the industry, apply them in your setting, and develop new skills for advancement in the field. Did you know that creating a professional development plan demonstrates to employees that you are invested in each of their success, and in return, they stay at your childcare center longer?

Organizing your childcare with a professional development plan not only strengthens your team, it reduces your recruiting and hiring expenses, while improving your company's culture. In fact, a 2020 Forbes article stated that over 77 percent of the

5,000 adults surveyed would consider a company's culture before applying for a job there, and half said company culture is more important than the salary.

A great way to grow into having an excellent company culture is by offering employees a say in their future at your childcare. Here are some things to consider in your professional development planning: Who, What, Where, When, and How.

Who: Who needs professional development training? Will the professional development training be geared towards specific individuals, the child care as a whole, or a targeted age group?

What: What level of knowledge are your teachers able to comprehend? Research the different areas of professional development training that your employees need to improve, know, or strengthen.

Where: Where are your teachers? Observe to see the level your employees are on (novice, intermediate, mastery). It's okay if they are on a different level, just make sure they are all benefiting from the professional development training.

When: When will professional development take place? Think about how quickly you need the professional development training completed. Are you trying to meet a deadline, is it based on growth, or job performance?

How: How will professional development be delivered? Consider the era that we live in. Will hands-on training be available, do you need to look into webinars, is there a hybrid model available, or a prerecorded professional development training such as Better Kid Care?

Not only do teachers need to attend professional development training, but they need to come back and teach it to those that didn't attend. Here are the things I needed them to take away from any training that they attended: **Reflect, Adapt, Implement.**

Reflect on the topic, and discuss two aha moments that were shared at the professional development training.

Adapt the information that was learned to their classroom environment including supervisor, co-teacher, and students.

Implement new knowledge within one week of the professional development so it can be put into practice.

This is how I made sure teachers were retaining information, and implementing it at the same time. All my teachers could fill any role from floater to director because of my professional development plan. I have teachers that have been with me for 7 out the 10 years that I have been in operation. I have teachers that have paid off debt because they applied the same level of standard to their personal life that they learned with me. So here are some practical steps that I use that can jumpstart your childcare today!

Two of the most game-changing strategies to better manage your program.

1: Hire smart from the start.

Try posing this question during your next interview:

Which statement would be appropriate to include in observational notes?

    a. "Bill made a mess while painting today."
    b. "Lois seems to be making a new friend."
    c. "Dan screamed when the clown approached."
    d. "Evan drank too much water at the playground."

What did that question have to do with your hiring process? EVERYTHING!! You do know you have to ask potential employees questions to check their mindset! They are either going to tell you what you want to hear or nothing at all, so you have to ask them questions to evaluate their potential. Plus, you are setting the standard for your childcare. Here, we don't manage our childcare on individual personal beliefs but beliefs that are going to set a standard and yield learning excellence. They will discount themselves if they don't feel like they can meet your expectations.

Also, this question is pulled directly from the Child Development Associate (CDA) Essential workbook. The CDA is a national credentialing program that is considered the best first step for employees entering the childcare industry. It's professional development training 101! Do not allow your staff to just put it away after they obtain the CDA. Continue to use it as a refresher in your monthly meetings. Even if it is not required in your county/state, you want to make sure your teachers are equipped with the early childhood knowledge, tools, and resources that they can gain from a great CDA class!

If your interview candidate did not get the question correct, there is no need to be discouraged. You can still hire them if they have all the attributes that you desire for a potential teacher. Just know they will need training in specific areas. With your new ongoing professional development plan, that should be no problem.

By the way, the answer to the question above is: C. Now, let us review the second strategy.

2: Create a succession plan.

The right person can become your successor if you train them right from the beginning. I get it. It is hard trusting someone, showing them all the ins and outs of your program, only for them to leave you high and dry. But you know what is even worse than that feeling? Burnout. Yes, that's right, burnout. You know, running on empty, fatigue, anxiety, panic attacks, feeling overwhelmed, overeating, high blood pressure. Does this describe you? If it does, well then, let's get you on the path of burn-out to breakthrough. A succession plan would be a great place to start after you take some much-needed time to yourself.

Succession is defined in the dictionary as: the action or process of inheriting a title, office, property, etc. I want you to get in the habit of thinking about the end first. What is your end result? I get it, not everyone wants to step away from their childcare and free up time. But there are some that do. With the end in mind, you can now go through the process of creating a succession plan. Just develop the plan. When the right person comes along to fill it, you will know. Here are some factors to consider as you think about your succession plan:

- Succession planning ensures leadership continuity.
- Develop your successor in ways that build their strengths.
- Concentrate resources on the development process to yield a return on your investment.
- Make sure you are personally involved in developing your successor.
- Hold yourself accountable.
- Your successor needs to be committed to their own self-development.
- Succession is linked to strategic planning and investment into the future.
- Leadership competencies are identified and used for development and selection of your successor.

So, let's recap. Early childhood education requires a grind that not everybody is born with. If you want to get your staff, teachers, or employees from A to Z, then you need a plan. Not just any plan, but a professional development plan. Creating a professional development training plan for your organization ensures company culture. Simply put, your company's culture is the community spirit, beliefs, and aspirations that have been manifested in the organization. Culture goes beyond the vibe, it impacts everything from recruitment and retention to performance. Remember that company culture influences every aspect of your business. Try writing down your company's core values, then set some company culture goals, include your whole team in the process, and most importantly, deliberately implement your company's culture ideas, best practices, and initiatives.

A smooth onboarding process will assist you in keeping up with your company's culture. Onboarding is how you integrate a new employee into your childcare. Have you noticed that employee turnover occurs in the first 45 days? That's because there is not a smooth onboarding process. I highly suggest that you add check marks into your system of operations. Try 30-day, 60-day, and 90-day meetings with the employee you are onboarding. Also, including the CDA in your interview process helps with the onboarding process. Stop looking at the CDA as one and done. Require your employees to bring their CDA professional portfolio to your meetings. Keeping them accountable by utilizing it as a resource will help them to stay at your facility longer.

Longevity is the name of the game. Employee retention can be crucial to any company but is especially important for child care businesses. Employee retention is your company's ability to retain employees. A strategy that can be used to retain employees is appreciating your employees. Whether it is catered lunches, discounted group purchases, or wellness offerings, appreciation can go a long way.

My favorite strategy is shaping employees' growth and development. Helping employees achieve their short-term and long-term goals is fulfilling and one of the most important employee retention strategies. Incorporating the CDA into your interview process and hiring smart from the start will save you heartache in the end. It will also prepare you for the next leg of your journey, which is succession planning. Successful program management plans with the end in mind. Invest in the future of your childcare program. What are you planning for? Your destiny is calling, are you ready to answer?

Checkout my action plan for professional development training, "The Destiny Plan," to get your teachers from hired to inspired: www.yourCDAsolutions.com

Chat With Me On:
Instagram @DiapersToDestiny
Facebook @Lizette Reid

ABOUT THE AUTHOR

Lizette Reid M.Ed., is an eminent and distinguished educator, professional development specialist, entrepreneur, speaker, and author. Her areas of expertise include; creating innovative learning experiences for early childhood professionals, childcare startups, verifying Child Development Associate (CDA)candidates, conducting First Aid/CPR training, and Sickle Cell Thalassemia awareness.

Lizette's educational journey started with her earning a Child Development Associate (CDA) while studying to obtain an Associate's Degree in Early Childhood Education. Then she completed the Director Credential while pursuing a Bachelor's Degree in Childcare Management. Lastly, she conquered the task of gaining a Masters Degree in Early Childhood Education while being married, raising a family, and managing a thriving childcare business.

During Lizette's 20 years in the Early Childhood Education field, she has been employed in every position in childcare as well as assisted in opening childcare facilities. In 2011, she became the CEO of her own child care facility. There she encourages children to grow to new heights daily through creative, and academic success.

Lizette has created engaging professional development training in bullying, embracing children's emotions, and cultural responsiveness that are listed on The Pennsylvania PD Registry. She has trained childcare bosses and leaders around the world with renowned Coach Andrea Dickerson and I Own A Daycare network. She has also presented with the CDA Council and Tennessee Early Childhood Training Alliance (TECTA). Lizette is currently an Adjunct Professor in Pennsylvania.

Higher learning has equipped Lizette with the tools needed to help others to succeed! The advanced training and over a decade of experience has enabled her to birth her consultant agency Diapers To Destiny! As the CEO of Diapers To Destiny Lizette is dedicated to STYLE! Helping childcare professionals reach **S**tandards **T**hat **Y**ield **L**earning **E**xcellence through the CDA!

IS IT REALLY TRUE?
IS IT REALLY, REALLY TRUE THAT YOU
CAN TURN STAFF INTO FAMILY?

Before starting this journey as a childcare center owner, I worked for the Detroit Public Schools system and had the opportunity to start an after-school program at one of their Pre-K thru Kindergarten buildings. My entrepreneurial dad, who has always taught me how to hustle, bought a building and asked, "What can we do with this building?" He suggested opening a laundromat, which I immediately dismissed, and I suggested a childcare center would be a great investment since I had been working in the field for a while. I felt like I could be of help to children before they entered kindergarten. People often ask me "did you start out of your home?" and I reply, "no"; but, in my mind, I'm thinking "Man, I wish that I had." I literally had to start from scratch.

I told you that my dad purchased a building, but what I did not tell you was that it was a run-down mechanic shop, then a church that wasn't even on record. Needless to say, a lot of work had to be done to the building, so I continued to work at DPS and we pumped a lot of money into it for renovations and to be honest, most of the work that was done was bootleg. Remember in the beginning I told you that my dad taught me how to hustle—that was because he was a hustler. Mr. Brown (my dad) knew how to rig just about anything. I thank God for his knowledge because I was able to pass the required inspections, and I was hoping that it would last. Well, you have to start somewhere. I continued to work for DPS because leaving wasn't an option. I had to use that income to pay for the daycare expenses, including payroll. I hired a director who happened to be someone that I ended up going to high school with, who just so happened to be looking for a job in childcare at that time.

How ironic, after a year, I got laid off from DPS, and my director ended up moving on to pursue her daycare dreams and goals, which I supported because I believe it is important to help people grow even if it's not with your company, and to this day, we still remain friends.

"Lead by example: Support women on their way to the top. Trust that they will extend a hand to those who follow."
~ Mariela Dabbah

My journey as an owner and director began, and boy did it begin. The staff I hired was only because we needed a body in the classroom and to meet licensing requirements; some staff had little or no experience in childcare, so you know how that turned out. Well, at that time, staff was coming and going, and

I knew that I couldn't provide quality care with all of the inconsistency. So, I said enough is enough: how can I get the teachers to stay? I realized my budget was limited, but I still needed high-quality staff, so I devised a plan to ensure low turnover.

I had to hire all new staff. The first place that I looked was at people who were around me, like those who I worked with at my previous job and the people in the community; not just the broad community, but I'm talking about people who would be able to walk to work. I wanted to help the community. I never really had to use employment sites to hire because I've always been able to hire on referrals or word of mouth, which is sometimes better because at least somebody knows them. I still have employees from the very beginning. Even when people disconnect from the village environment, they still come to our gatherings and events with open arms.

Now this is funny! I have this one staff member that I interviewed on a Friday, but just so happened to be at the same party that I attended, the very next day. She said, "Oh my God," to her now husband, "I just interviewed with that lady," and then she started to duck and dodge me the rest of the night. She later said to me "I did not want you to look at me differently." I didn't look at her in any negative way; in fact, I ended up hiring her.

It is important to know a little about what your staff's life is like outside of work. Now this is going to be mind blowing, because that same staff member I actually had to change her work schedule three times. She was hired for the 8:00 AM work schedule, but as time went on she was constantly late, so I asked her if 8:30 AM would be a better time, and to my surprise, that still didn't work. I had a candid conversation with her to figure out what would work, and we came up with 9:00 AM, and she has been working that schedule ever since. I learned from this that you have to meet people where they are and show compassion in order to work with them. Now some people are not worth working with, but she was, so having discernment is important as well. I love being a small business owner because it allows me to have more control with helping people. Realizing the need to be more accommodating with schedules for staff, I ended up implementing a 4-day work week, which gave them an opportunity to have a day off to handle all of their personal business on their time, not mine. As a result, it reduced staff from calling off and getting burned out, and gave them an opportunity to get some rest and have more time with their family.

"I wish more women realized that helping another woman win, cheering her on, praying for her, or sharing a resource with her, does not take away from the blessings coming to them. In fact, the more you give, the more you receive. Empowering women doesn't come from selfishness but rather from selflessness."
~ Selena Kinder

My goal is to build a relationship with my employees. I want my employees to see me as more than someone who signs their paycheck and a micro-manager. After all, I spend more time with my staff than anyone else, so I never want to have a superficial relationship with them. I want them to feel comfortable and I want to build trust; I need them to believe in my vision, which is our vision. I have lunch with them in the staff lounge. We have quarterly team building events. I make sure birthdays are recognized. Anniversaries are celebrated and we have an annual Christmas party, and gifts are given throughout the year.

I'm constantly hearing that there should be boundaries between the boss and the employees. Down through the years, I realized I can be a better leader than a boss. Don't get it twisted, boundaries are necessary; my staff knows I am the boss and not their BFF. There was this one employee who tested my leadership often. I've learned sometimes people are just not assigned to you (thanks Coach), so the outcome will not be the same for them. I had a staff member, the youngest staff member of the group. I knew she needed to be groomed for the job because she came to me right after high school, and I tried to work with her over the years because she was my son's age, so I knew the struggle that generation was going through (the kids that were given everything). However, for some reason, that family approach was not working with her; once again, don't get it twisted, I'm friendly, yes, but BFF, no!

Unfortunately, due to being disrespectful and trying to test my authority, I had to let her go, but it wasn't with an "okay, thank you for the opportunity" departure. It was with a negative cursing me out text departure; that hurt me to my core. There was Facebook bashing, and mostly all of the comments were from people who didn't even know the many chances that were given to this person over the years. And yes, I got comments from other childcare owners saying "girl, I told you, you can't get close to them. They will turn on you in a minute." I said to myself and to some close colleagues, "I will never treat staff like family again," but God said to my spirit, **"don't get weary in doing well, for in due season I will reap if I don't faint"** (**Galatians 6:9**). I learned not to let one apple spoil the bunch, so I got over that situation, and continued to show love and respect to my staff, as if nothing happened. I am cautious and aware of my boundaries now. Since then, I have gained an employee that is the perfect fit for that classroom. The overall morale of my remaining staff has improved, all because one bad apple was removed from the bunch.

"Your greatest test will be how you handle people who mishandled you."

Understand that nothing is personal; you need to practice this with your staff. If you must reprimand your staff and you have a good relationship with them, more than likely they won't take it personally because they have developed thick skin and value your decision. Remind yourself, "Don't take it personally, it's just business."

Remember, even in a family structure everybody can't go with you. God will remove people out of your business and life who are not divinely connected to you and your vision.

As the founder of Village of Shiny Stars (VOSS) Childcare Center, I have over 15 years of experience implementing successful methods for retaining employees. In the childcare industry, new hires are costly if you take into consideration the time and expense of background checks, uniforms, drug tests, training, and all the other elements associated with the hiring process. Although I retained professional boundaries, my strategy created a comfortable environment for my staff as well as me. One of my key retention strategies is treating my team like family instead of employees.

Outcome

Team continuity builds stronger work-related relationships and provides greater comfort and stability for the children. Additionally, parents are pleased and make note of staff consistency. Other business owners recognized my success and began to ask about my methods. Then it became my goal to help childcare centers retain their staff after the hiring process. Treating my staff like family instead of employees has enabled me to keep my costs down and retain my staff longer.

As a result of my methods, I have 15 years of continuous business with a retention rate of 80%. One of my employees has been with me for 14 years, and the average team member stays at least 8 years. Not only that, but in regularly distributed surveys, my team consistently reports they are happy and pleased with their jobs at VOSS, which is proven by their decision to stay.

According to employeepedia.com:

"It takes a lot of time and energy to build a great employee and only a second to lose one. Do not expect your employees to exceed the expectations of your customers if you do not exceed yours as the management. Make the other person feel important and do it with a sincere heart."

Below you will find my nine step "Retention Matters Method." My method will help you retain and build relationships with the right staff for your childcare business:

Method 1. Incorporate policies and procedures so the team understands expectations. This can be done by:

- Offering a written guide
- Offering regular training sessions and quizzes
- Doing roleplay
- Providing training videos

Method 2. Train your staff so they are effective. This can be done by:

- Having professional development days that go through the work day from open to close
- Providing mock exercises
- Offering quarterly/monthly meetings for training sessions
- Offering training videos that are mobile app compliant
- Providing a staff retreat

Method 3. Ensure management is interactive so the team feels supported.

- Management should be present and actively participating in day-to-day activities
- Management should assist the staff
- Ensure staff has all the materials and supplies required to do the job
- Nothing should catch the director off guard

Method 4. Show your staff that you value them by being mindful of their needs and interests.

- Reward hard work
- Have one-on-one meetings to see how they are doing
- Listen to your staff
- Offer open communication
- Determine the staff's interests and hobbies and incorporate that in the center

Method 5. Build a strong team that will work together toward your vision.

This can be done by:

- Ensuring the team knows the vision; Include the vision in the handbook
- Posting your vision on the wall at your center
- Having team building exercises
- Being inclusive

Method 6. Reward good work so the staff feels appreciated.

This can be done by:

- Acknowledging creativity, hard work, and tasks well done
- Buying the staff breakfast/lunch/dinner
- Giving out bonuses
- Celebrating anniversaries with gifts
- Having employee recognition days
- Celebrating your team by having employee of the month

Method 7. Show compassion by being understanding.

This can be done by:

- Being honest
- Being transparent
- Listening
- Putting yourself in their shoes

Method 8. Lead by example not by your ego.

This can be done by:

- Holding yourself to the same standards
- Acknowledging your own mistakes
- Looking in the mirror
- Being humble
- Not being above doing any job in your business

Method 9. Show appreciation

This can be done by:

- Rewarding your team
- Giving your team gifts
- Verbalizing your appreciation
- Celebrating special days like birthdays, holidays, etc.
- Stocking staff lounge with goodies and coffee maker
- Having teacher appreciation week

In summary, the struggle to find and keep staff is real, especially during the pandemic where the applicants are slim to none, and with people not showing up to interviews, we have to change the way we see and treat our staff; they are the ones who hold our business together.

I want you to take one of the methods I gave you above and focus on that one method for 30 days. You will find that you will build trust and an unbreakable bond with your staff.

If you would like more information or to grab my new release book, Retention Matters, please contact me at:

Email: villagestars@yahoo.com

Website: www.villageofshinystars.net

ABOUT THE AUTHOR

Sonya Hickey is an educator, lifelong learner, wife, mother and true boss lady! Sonya was born and raised in the city of Detroit where she attended Detroit Public Schools. Her childcare business is located in the City of Detroit. She is a former Detroit Public Schools (DPS) teacher, and her last assignment was working in an early childhood building which inspired her to open her own childcare center in 2006. She not only enjoys working with children/families, but she also loves working alongside her staff. Sonya serves in the Children's ministry at her church serving children ages 2 years old to 12. She has also provided onsite childcare for local parent cafes, so parents could participate without the need to find a baby-sitter elsewhere.

Sonya holds a Master of Arts degree in Education and is the owner and director of Village of Shiny Stars Child Care Center serving children and families from birth to 12 years old. Since opening in 2016, Village of Shiny Stars has served over 1000 children and their families. We offer Early Head Start, Great Start Readiness Program (GSRP), and latchkey services. The partnership with GSRP has been for nearly 7 years and nearly 6 years with Early Head Start. With over 15 years of successfully owning and operating VOSS, Sonya has positioned VOSS as a successful and profitable entity with many satisfied customers and demands for expansion and a second location in Inkster, Michigan

VOSS participated in the Great Start Collaborative Wayne pilots for local Quality Rating Improvement System when the program launched, and Sonya served on the planning committee. This work was critical in forming Michigan's QRIS system. VOSS currently has a 4-star rating, per the State of Michigan QRIS.

Sonya is the former President and co-founder of 'Rising Advocates for Young Children', in which Rising provided a Basic Needs pantry for families housed in the garage of Village of Shiny Stars. Families were given access to the pantry on a monthly basis while also providing eye opening field trips for

BQI students since 2016. The organization consisted of several other childcare providers, in the Brightmoor community .

She created an orientation for youth to be able to work in the childcare centers in Brightmoor. She spoke at a Michigan State Capitol hearing to testify regarding the process of parents billing for childcare providers.

Sonya is currently participating with Providers for Change and in October 2020 we were able to share our concerns at the State Capital. Sonya is a member of the newly constructed advocate group Early Childhood Empowerment Collaborative which advocates for resources to benefit early childhood in Michigan. Sonya is a member of the Association of Early Childhood Leaders and Jump Start Bosses of America. Sonya participates regularly on a Child Care providers morning prayer call by I Own A Daycare. Sonya is a former member of the Childcare Success Summit through Kris Murray. Sonya participates in various leadership and professional development conferences both in State and out of State centered around Early Childhood Education.

Sonya has been a recipient of several grants. A Skillman Foundation grant which allowed her to visit and observe Bank Street in New York and Ounce prevention in Chicago. She received the supporting Brightmoor Leaders Grant, in which she was able to attend a conference of her choice with her staff leadership team. In 2019, she was awarded a grant to plan and host the 1st Annual Early Childhood Summit for local childcare business directors and owners called "Nothing Personal; It's just Business", which was a huge success with 60 participants. The next Summit is tentatively scheduled for later this year. Sonya participates in the Brightmoor Quality Initiative (BQI). She is a recipient of the IFF learning spaces grant and the City of Detroit Motor City Restore program.

Mrs. Hickey is a solid pillar in the community, providing quality early childhood services and programs to the Brightmoor Community where she has worked diligently with local community leaders, partners, and sister childcare providers to bring early childhood resources.

Her best kept secret is the release of her new book titled: Retention Matters. You can grab your copy by heading over to www.villageofshinystars.net

THE FINANCIAL
METHOD

THE 7-SECRETS TO FINANCIAL HEALING BIBLICAL PRINCIPLES

-Do you have any debt?

-Do you feel you are on track to be debt-free at this point in your life?

-Do you have any assets to protect?

-Do you have a will, trust & powers of attorney in place to protect your assets and children?

-Do you have your personal and financial information organized and readily available in case of an emergency?

-Do you have identity theft protection?

-Do you have a 750+ credit score that can save you the most money and give you the most control?

-Do you have the proper life insurance coverage for your family?

-Do you have a retirement portfolio in place?

Anyone who answers "no" to any of these questions would benefit greatly by changing their financial lifestyle to live it within my 7 secrets of financial freedom. I have been using the system taught by Dave Ramsey, the 7 baby steps, within the Financial Peace University program, and I am a certified Ramsey preferred coach. I have been using this system of personal growth and self-improvement for over five years. I have taught this system to a diverse population. I have used it with people of all ages, creeds, color, professions, and socio-economic status. My financial system has even proven effective for the nation and they reported effective results.

THE 7-SECRETS MODEL

My 7-SECRETS model system has at its core three biblical keys that are the foundation of my secrets.

Biblical Key #1-GIVING AND RECEIVING

"Give, and it will be given unto you; good measure, pressed down, and shaken together, and running over, shall men give into your bosom. For with the same measure that ye meet withal it shall be measured to you again." (LUKE 6:38, KJV)

"But this I say, He which soweth sparingly shall reap also sparingly; and he which soweth bountifully shall reap also bountifully." (2 CORINTHIANS 9:6, KJV)

These scriptures do not paint a picture of lack but rather paint a picture of "ABUNDANCE" and "PLENTY." It is clear when we give, we can expect a return.

Biblical Key #2-KINGDOM CONCERN

"Therefore take no thought, saying, What shall we eat? or, What shall we drink? or, Wherewithal shall we be clothed? (For after all these things do the Gentile seek:) for your heavenly Father knoweth that ye have need of all these things. But seek ye first the kingdom of God, and his righteousness; and all these things shall be added unto you." (MATTHEW 6:31-33, KJV)

How many of us worry about money? Worry means to "allow one's mind to dwell on difficulty or troubles." Jesus teaches us in this verse not to worry. How do we avoid worry or at least minimize worry in life? "Focus on the Kingdom of God." Focus on the true treasure. Focus on the true vision. Focus on the true master. Focus on the purpose of life.

Biblical Key #3-WORK

"He becometh poor that dealeth with slack hand: but the hand of the diligent maketh rich." (Proverbs 10:4, KJV)

"In all labour there is profit: but the talk of the lips tendeth only to penury." (Proverbs 14:23, KJV)
When you go to work and work hard, you can enjoy the fruit of your labor. Develop an excellent work ethic and you will achieve wealth.

THE 7-SECRETS SYSTEM TO FINANCIAL HEALING

Secret 1. TITHING AND OFFERING

"And Melchizedek king of Salem brought forth bread and wine: and he was the priest of the most high God. And he blessed him, and said, Blessed be Abram of the most high God, possessor of heaven and earth: And blessed be the most high God, which hath delivered thine enemies into thy hand. And he gave him tithes of all." (GENESIS 14:18-20, KJV)

The first secret we need to examine is the principle of Tithe. The word Tithe means 1/10th or 10%. Abram's act of obedience in giving a Tithe of everything started the process of God's Blessings and eventually being blessed with the promise seed Isaac. This was also an act of WORSHIP. Now understand, Abram was not just giving to Melchizedek but was also giving them to God through the office of the priest.

Secret 2. INVEST IN TO YOURSELF FIRST

The problem I have learned over the years is at the end of the month, most people don't have anything left to save. My consideration at the first of the month, before you pay anything, write a check or direct deposit to yourself for 10% of your income. Paying yourself first may be the single most important secret in this lesson. "Remember, it's not what you earn, it's what you keep!" Learn to put yourself at the head of the line. Treat your savings plan like a recurring bill that is necessary each month to pay. Dedicate the appropriate amount each month and set it aside. Change your mindset and build a savings plan for your financial future. Another part of investing into yourself is purchasing products or resources that can help you self-develop in your expertise. My consideration is to invest into books, audio downloads, coaches, and information needed to help you become financially healed.

Secret 3. MINDSET SHIFT CONCERNING MONEY

The way we think about money means everything. Your mindset is a powerful thing, especially when it comes to what you believe about money. After working with many clients concerning their finances, I have found their victories and losses were due to the way they were thinking. Many people win the lottery and end up losing it all, then we have many people become self-made millionaires. What is the difference in the two groups? It's how they think. If you think you do not deserve to be financially secure, you'll never be financially secure. However, if you "upgrade" your self-image and believe you deserve the freedom and peace of mind that financial freedom provides, you will have more of a chance of obtaining wealth beyond your dreams.

SECRET 4. ADJUST YOUR LIFESTYLE

Under this secret, the major key and point is "get on a budget!" Adjusting your priorities can come with the tough rule of life. You cannot have everything at one time, but you can get to the place where you can live like no one else, purchase what you want, give like you want, and be financially free. You will have to make conscious decisions based on a budget about every purchase.

AN IMPORTANT CONCEPT TO UNDERSTAND IS WANT VS. NEED:

-A need is something you have to have, something you cannot do without. For example, we need food, shelter, and the basic utilities.

-A want is something you desire to have, like a brand-new Mercedes Benz, and not considering the finance charge, monthly cost, and most of all, the maintenance for the vehicle. If you want to achieve financial freedom, you may have to make sacrifices for a period of time and go without some of your wants. It's not that tough, but it is very, very important to your financial healing.

SECRET 5. ESTABLISH A BUDGET

I believe budgeting is the best way to take control of your spending. When you set a plan before the first of the month to set a budget, it will determine what you will spend on certain items, and sticking to a plan can make a world of difference in where your money goes. Budgeting is also a great way to determine where you're wasting money. I will consider it as a family exercise, and keep a budget for one month. Try not to make it so much trouble you won't keep it up; just a rough record will do. Develop an envelope system of keeping cash in it and record along with your receipt every expense. Use a sheet or even a legal pad for the record. I guarantee you at the end of the month, you'll have a real eye opener. You will be amazed at how the little things can add up to big dollars! The main purpose of a budget is this: it gives you full control of your own money. I promise you there's nothing quite as good as the feeling that you are in control of your money, rather than your money and expenses controlling you.

SECRET 6. AVOID THE CREDIT AND DEBT TRAP

I have found in my personal life and assisting my coaching clients, credit cards are good for convenience, but that's it. You must be careful to avoid the pitfalls of plastic money. Pay your balance in full each month and you'll not only avoid interest charges but you'll prevent your balance from escalating out of control. To keep your monthly charges under control, use my advice in the last section under establishing a budget, pay with cash. You'll find you spend less when you have to hand your money over in the form of cash. When you spend a Benjamin, $100.00 bill, you feel that more than swiping your credit card. Study your options, for you do have a choice concerning your financial future.

Next, generate a plan to pay off all debt and avoid financing or borrowing any more money. The rich ruleth over the poor, and the borrower is servant to the lender (Proverbs 22:7, KJV). Out of all the threats to your financial security, none is more dangerous than debt. In every family's quest for financial freedom, debt is the most common enemy. Be careful of the thoughts, or your uncle who is not financially free, telling you we will always have debt, for that is not true. You do not have to accept it. Those types of thoughts are what makes debt one of the biggest threats to your financial well-being.

Revolving debt vs. Fixed debt. Credit card debt is known as revolving debt. The interest compounds daily instead of monthly, which means you can pay much more interest. Maybe you are wondering why? Because with revolving debt, unlike with fixed debt, there is no fixed amount that you pay each month, your debt can go on forever. Again, pay your debt as soon as possible and you can use the debt stacking method, which I can teach you if you decide to coach with me.

SECRET 7. EARN ADDITIONAL INCOME

We have come to the final secret of the seven principles in which I live by and use to earn more money. You have many options to earn more income: get a part-time job, start a side hustle business, or if you are in business, create another stream of income. Your family income may be very modest, and things may be so tight that it is tough to invest more than $50-$100 a month. Again, consider making more money in order to save more and pay off debt faster. I am not saying it will be easy, but a little hard work has never hurt anybody. And, believe me, the rewards are worth it. Also, consider the whole family picking up extra work, for there is nothing wrong with the children working also. Listen, everyone must know the family is on a mission to experience financial freedom. "All hands on deck!" When you learn to implement these ideas, you will find financial healing and peace being a part of your life and family.

There you have it. These are the seven secrets for financial healing and real financial freedom. I have been coaching clients individually and in group sessions for several years now, and I am encouraged to know that by implementing these secrets, you will experience the same victories they did.

My final thoughts, "START NOW!" Problem: If you don't start now, you may never reach financial independence. Solution: Begin today to apply the fundamentals, teach them to your family, and start a tradition that you can pass on for generations to come. A good man leaveth an inheritance to his children's children: and the wealth of the sinner is laid up for the just (Proverbs 13:22, KJV). If you want to build financial freedom, it is essential that you begin your plan as soon as possible. The principles we've talked about in this section of this powerful book will put you on the right track towards financial healing and financial independence, which will bless your entire generation.

ABOUT THE AUTHOR

Kamau J. Dickerson, Certified Financial Coach, is the owner of Financial Healing Coaching LLC, and pastor of Unity of the Bridegroom Church, Brunswick, GA and Immanuel House of Prayer United, Darien, GA. Pastor Dickerson's passion is to help eliminate poverty and help people achieve financial freedom through being healed financially, mentally, physically, emotionally, and spiritually. He has developed The 7 Secrets to Financial Healing to assist his clients with achieving their desired Goals and Dreams. Pastor Dickerson is a financial coach and financial educator and provides financial literacy advice for clients, in particular, childcare business owners, all over the nation. He conducts training programs and workshops for small businesses and organizations in retirement investments, taxes, money management, life insurance, credit education, and estate planning.

Kamau holds a Financial Mastery Certification with Dave Ramsey Solutions, Graduate and Licensed for the State of GA in life insurance and annuities, certified in financial literacy training. He has worked in co-ownership with his wife, Coach Andrea Dickerson, for the past several years as the CFO of their corporation. Kamau holds several certifications in financial education, leadership development, and theological studies. He is the author of *Childcare Success Principles For Men: 5 Must-Know Secrets to Causing Increase in Life and Business*. Pastor Dickerson's motto is, "The Difference Between A Moment And Movement Is Sacrifice!" Therefore, financial healing is not a moment for him, but a movement.

Pastor Kamau Dickerson can be contacted at:

-Financial Healing Coaching LLC

3312 Norwich Street, Brunswick, Georgia 31520

-financialhealingcoaching.com

-IOwnadaycare.com

-912-222-1313

THE MILLION DOLLAR
SYSTEM

THE BEGINNING TO MY
MILLION DOLLAR SYSTEM

Hey, guys. This is your coach, Andrea Dickerson, here with IOwnADaycare.com. Today, I want to share with you my story that happened in my childcare business. It was a historic moment for me. The reason why I say it was historic is because I figured out what makes and breaks a business. This date was noted in my business history! I remember it just like yesterday, I went into my childcare business and I realized that I wasn't serving my ideal client.

I was literally shocked. I was shocked that I had parents that weren't appreciative of the work that I put in for my proprietary systems. It took me twelve months to build my brand and business around a 30-day potty training system and my See It, Say It, Master It curriculum. However, with this curriculum, I needed parents that would value doing the work at home, and these parents were not doing the work at home.

It was just too hard for me to enjoy the labor and sacrifices that it takes for anyone to operate a quality learning childcare program. I wanted to be valued because I had built my own proprietary curriculum.

Week by week, lesson by lesson, date by date, number by number, alphabet by alphabet, skill by skill, I could go on and on, but you get my point. It took me time, research, and some!

That meant I had a program that was built from scratch, blood, sweat, and tears!

My curriculum is built around the Law of Affirmation. I teach our children sight words by using a biblical law of Affirmation, seeing it, saying it, and mastering it.

However, if parents were not working with their children at home and turning in the homework, there was no way our children would succeed. I became very unhappy because I wasn't seeing my children evolve.

Let me explain to you the importance of creating a curriculum and your own learning processes and standards. Please remember, when you purchase your curriculum, it is in your best interest to organize your curriculum in such a way that it is easy for your teachers, parents, and our children to follow your system and track their effort and be held accountable. I created a ten-week curriculum system that every child from ages 18 months and up would learn from. My process included 8 learning domains over 10 consecutive weeks and then on the 11th week, they would have assessments and a report card. It's very hard to explain; however, I created a video just for you with my breakdown of my curriculum semester schedule. Check out the video here>>>>>

This curriculum system is highly effective because by the 12th week, our teachers would have received training to support the next 12 weeks of curriculum plans for our children.

What a great learning system, right? So why was it that I had the wrong parents?

Here's what happened. A Million-Dollar System In The Wrong Hands. That's what happened. I left my business and watched the money. The money was working, but the branding was changing. How was the branding changing?

I realized that there were a few things that were missing during our parent orientation and also during the marketing process. Your parent interaction means everything to your branding and success. For instance, when the parents walked in to take a tour, I realized our program features weren't discussed. They trusted the faces of the employees and not the program features; many of the parents couldn't care less. Suddenly, after going into my center and interacting at the front desk, I realized, oh man, I'm not marketing to my ideal client. Something has to change.

I was literally shocked the moment I walked in. It happens every day in childcare, so be careful, watch out for serving parents that just need childcare. I got caught up in that cycle, and when the director and eight other staff members quit and went with the director, the parents that were currently enrolled didn't need what I offered. What really shocked me was the fact that I knew I had a million-dollar system and I left it in the wrong hands and was serving the wrong client.

I literally have a million-dollar childcare system. I can take my system and go to any city anywhere, use my same systems, my same mindset, my same strategies, my same marketing, and dominate.

My epiphany moment happened rather slowly. Years later, I realized that if I service the right parent who appreciates what I offer, marketing for me will be easy because they're going to know families that want what I have. They're going to know more families that want quality and affordable childcare services.

SECRET#1 Client Attraction

I got up from my director seat and I started managing my centers from home. I didn't keep my hands involved in my everyday operations like I should have.

When that shocking moment came to me, I did what a lot of you all need to do. I then pulled out my Client Attraction Trigger System. This system helps you to hone in on the ideal client you desire to serve. It helps me to think about the places they go, how to create my message to speak to them, and it causes me to dream about what I want my ideal client to look like. This is called the client attraction way. All of the gurus that I had been learning under and all the marketing material I had been learning from taught me client attraction and what that really looks like. I realized, wait a minute, this is not happening in my company. I'm not where I want to be or marketing to my ideal client in my company. Then I started saying, okay, help me attract the right marketing client.

That's when I started doing billboards. I started creating a marketing message about our 30-day potty training system. The reason behind it all was I wanted parents that valued our system. I wanted parents that valued that if you bring your child to us, they'll be potty trained within 30 days.

Then I started training my teachers more intentionally, having trainings with them at the eleventh week of a curriculum week. I would pull them out of their classroom and bring them over to my corporate office.

I started better servicing my staff by training them intentionally on my curriculum. I'm also training my staff intentionally on potty training. Why? Because this is my million-dollar system.

This is the system that worked for my academy. Many of you are trying to market your company the way everybody else markets, when you have to get intentional about your ideal client. What is it that they want?

Let me tell you guys how I found out what my ideal client wanted. When I had this shocking moment, the best way I knew how was to observe people in my community, ask the right questions during my tour, and think about the biggest employer in my city, and how I was going to get to that market. I knew I wanted a two-parent household. I knew I wanted a certain income medium. That was because in marketing, they teach you what percentage of a person's income can be utilized for different services. I knew that with childcare, there was a particular percentage. Based on research, this percentage was ten percent.

Once I did that percentage, I was like, okay, I need to make sure that I'm attracting the clients that can afford this percentage of income. Sure enough, it started happening. We started getting parents from the hospital because when I first opened up, these people were immediately attracted to me and my marketing; however, it was once I started growing, and I lifted my hands off of my operations, and I didn't focus as much as I should have. It was too easy. I just started figuring that people were coming because they liked the staff that was working for me instead of the brand.

SECRET #2 The Brand.

You want to attract people that like your brand. It doesn't matter what teachers show up as long as your brand continues to deliver the same service over and over again. That's why parents need to show up, because they like your brand, not because of your teachers, not because of the people, but your brand.

Branding is so essential. Grab your flyers and review them. Now ask yourself, what is the one thing that your childcare business can do well without skipping a beat? Don't think that the smallest deliverable such as a hot meal is normal. Nowadays, it's not normal. Don't overthink it. Hey, if you need my help, text me Jumpstart to 484848. By texting me, I can teach you more about branding. Now, back to the lesson. To build my brand, I began by gathering the right marketing message from listening to my clients, following my heart, and improving my marketing headlines.

I created my Client Attraction Trigger System. This Client Attraction Trigger System can be found at www.childcaremadeeasy.com. To accomplish this, I go through this manifestation process. I go through the process of identifying my ideal client. I sit quietly and research the market and use the information that I gathered and go through the process of identifying where they work, what they read, where they go to school, and their monthly income. I wrote all of that down.

The reason behind this is because this is the part that requires the work. Whenever you have gone through a manifestation process, it's good to visualize. After you visualize, you've got to wake up and do the work. This is the work part. The work part was for me to keep my mind focused on who I was marketing to, my marketing message, my marketing strategy, my ideas to reach those clients, and the results that I get from my marketing. The reason why is because I write results as if I'm successful, as if it has already happened, like it's already done.

Here's an example: When I started to see a reduced number of enrollments for my childcare center, I went to my Facebook profile and downloaded all of the pictures of the parents I desired to service. Once I obtained the pictures, I placed them on my Client Attraction Cards. Then I started doing the work by going to their jobs and reaching out so that I can come in and provide presentations and share the benefits of the parents using my daycare and increase the company's retention rate. Check out the flyer I used to hand out to the employers.

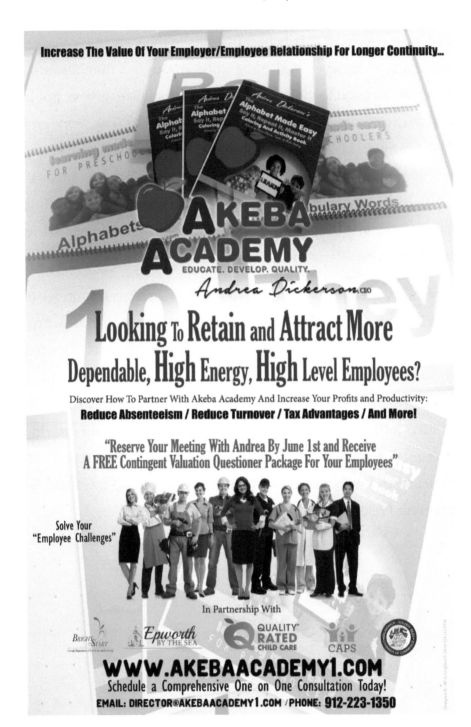

Next, I am ready to use the ideal client avatar research and create my billboard content. I rarely ever leave my billboard content up to my billboard sales rep. I know childcare and marketing, they know sales.

Let me really say it the best way I know how, It's MY billboard marketing piece, I didn't depend on the billboard organization to give me a marketing message. First of all, if we're doing that, ladies, we're wrong. The reason why is because billboard people sell billboards; they don't sell childcare. They don't know how your marketing message needs to be.

I started with asking a question on my billboard, NEED HELP WITH POTTY TRAINING? Check out my billboard marketing piece below:

What I did was I asked a simple question on my billboard. I used the colors black, and white, and yellow because I found out through studies that those colors are the most attractive image or the most attractive colors that stop the riders and passersby, and that causes the car drivers to look and to focus. I started moving in that direction with the right colors on my billboard and then having the right marketing message, something as simple as "Need help with potty training?" Anybody riding past that billboard and they need help with potty training, that automatically catches their eye.

I literally had grandparents coming in and buying my *Potty Helper* book. They weren't enrolling; they were just buying my *Potty Helper* book. I had parents that were enrolling for the 30 days just to get the potty training help. This really diversified my culture of parents.

At one time, our parents were majority black women. Then, by changing my marketing message, I started attracting white women, Hispanic women, and single fathers. The fathers who weren't good with potty training their daughters, they would come and they would show up because they needed help with potty training. Did you all catch that?

That's what I did, but it took for me to go through this Client Attraction Trigger System. It took for me to go through the manifestation process. Then it took for me to do the behind the scene work. The behind the scene work was creating a marketing message that will work for my clients.

Listen, ladies, if you are interested in my process of what I went through, purchase your Client Attraction Trigger System. It's a game changer. It makes you think. Now, you have to be a thinker; you have to be a strategist. You have to know that this is the right thing to do for your company.

You can't just rely on word of mouth; you can't just rely on what has happened in your past. Some of us are living off of generational wealth. Some of us own childcare businesses that our parents built.

Your mom built that; your uncle built that; your grandparents built that. You're living off of what they have built. You don't really know childcare; you just came into a done-for-you business and if that's the case, it's time to make this personal and be determined to know more and grow more!

ABOUT THE AUTHOR

Listen, if you're wanting to utilize a principle that will keep your business moving forward, that principle will create your million-dollar system.

Create it for the ideal client and keep going for the ideal client, and you'll find yourself where you want to be in your childcare business. All right, head over to my website, www.IOwnADaycare.com.

Andrea Dickerson
Childcare Systems Queen
I Help Childcare Owners Create Systematized 6 and 7 Figure Childcare Business Models.